Advance praise for *Advice Worth Ignoring*

"If you only read one parenting book this year, make it this one. Dr. Ray dismantles all of the misguided ideas about parenting that flood our society today, and leaves you with commonsense wisdom that makes you feel calm, equipped, and excited to face your day as a parent. When you're done with this book, you'll feel as if a huge weight has been taken from your shoulders."

—JENNIFER FULWILER
radio host, bestselling author, and mom of six

"In *Advice Worth Ignoring,* Dr. Ray continues to provide parents with ideas on how to raise children who will love them and love God. Unlike many 'experts' whose only experience with children seems to derive from case studies, Ray has raised ten kids (or, as he says, his wife has, since he has been busy writing books on raising kids). His experiences with his own children are not only insightful but also heartwarming, making this book instructive, charming, and fun to read!"

—DR. MARY KAY CLARK
director, Seton Home Study School

"*Advice Worth Ignoring* is a reassuring handbook for Catholic parents who want to raise their children to become confident and compassionate adults. Dr. Ray presents answers to many of the most pressing questions about how to identify and resist cultural messages that are based not on Catholic values but on pop psychology, and which have the potential to undermine parents and tear apart families."

—THOMAS S. MONAGHAN
founder of Domino's Pizza, Ave Maria University,
and Ave Maria School of Law

"Dr. Ray is a voice of reason in what is often an unreasonable time. He offers insight and hope for the daunting job of parenting with advice that takes into account our children's spiritual well-being, not just behavior modification. He makes us laugh, think, and reach for the best in us."

—ROSE MALAVOLTI
professional educator, speaker,
and mother of twenty-one children

Advice Worth Ignoring

HOW TUNING OUT THE EXPERTS CAN MAKE YOU A BETTER PARENT

DR. RAY GUARENDI

Trust good
sense!

Ray.

servant

AN IMPRINT OF
FRANCISCAN MEDIA
Cincinnati, Ohio

Cover design by LUCAS Art & Design
Cover image © Masterfile
Book design by Mark Sullivan

Library of Congress Cataloging-in-Publication Data
Names: Guarendi, Ray, author.
Title: Advice worth ignoring : how tuning out the experts can make you a better parent / Dr. Ray Guarendi.
Description: Cincinnati : Servant, 2016.
Identifiers: LCCN 2016015997
Subjects: LCSH: Parenting—Religious aspects—Christianity—Miscellanea. | Child rearing—Religious aspects—Christianity—Miscellanea. | Common fallacies—Miscellanea.
Classification: LCC BV4529 .G83 2016 | DDC 248.8/45—dc23
LC record available at https://lccn.loc.gov/2016015997

ISBN 978-1-63253-132-2

Published by Servant,
an imprint of Franciscan Media
28 W. Liberty St.
Cincinnati, OH 45202
www.FranciscanMedia.org

Printed in the United States of America.
Printed on acid-free paper.
16 17 18 19 20 5 4 3 2 1

─::::: CONTENTS :::::─

My Advice about Advice

Smart people learn from their mistakes. Smarter people learn from the mistakes of others. The smartest people learn from good advice.

A pithy observation. Also, it would seem, good advice. No one learns solely from his own experience. If he tried, he'd find life a lot more frustrating, and perhaps a lot shorter. All of us learn, for better or worse, by others' guidance. The aim is to get better at separating good guidance from bad.

Some years ago I was a guest on a TV talk show about oppositional adolescents. A mother of rebellious teens challenged me, "Do you have any children?"

"Yes," I replied, "I have six." (That was our family size at the time.)

Not to be upstaged, she countered with, "Are any of them teenagers?"

"Not yet," I answered, prompting her "checkmate" expression. Clearly, she believed that to give someone helpful counsel, you need to have worn her shoes (or, in this case, raised teenaged kids).

Really? I am not a child of divorce, a troubled adolescent, addicted to drugs, or (as far as I am aware) mentally ill. Neither am I an octogenarian, atheist, or woman. If my practice were limited to subjects with which I have direct, personal experience, I would pretty much be limited to seeing clients who are middle-aged white males, married for thirty years to the same wife, with ten kids (the updated number).

Am I saying that experience is not helpful for giving good advice? Of course not. Listening to the experiences of parents who have gone through similar situations, or talking to doctors and therapists who can present options you might not have thought of, makes good sense. But blindly following the advice of others is a bad idea—it can undercut your confidence and authority as a parent. Here are a few examples.

Advice by numbers. The journalist Edward R. Murrow said: "Just because your voice reaches halfway around the world, doesn't mean you are any wiser than when it reached only to the end of the bar."

Mr. Murrow might have trouble convincing people of his wisdom today. In our media-saturated society, numbers lend credibility. The more ears hearing a voice, the more trustworthy the source is perceived to be—whether that audience is reached through the airwaves, in print, or through cyberspace.

Whether I'm talking only to my neighbor lady or to a million-plus like her, the size of the crowd holding a certain opinion of me (good or bad) is not in and of itself a reliable indicator of the soundness of my advice. Indeed, some of history's most destructive ideas gained traction because they targeted and were absorbed by large audiences.

To quote Bishop Fulton Sheen: "Wrong is wrong even if everybody is wrong. Right is right even if nobody is right." The words of highly rated TV parenting gurus are not secular gospel because they have a large market share.

Advice by letters. Educated doesn't always mean *smart.* And yet, for many people, the number of letters following someone's name exponentially increases the perceived soundness of his or her expertise.

Don't misread me. I am not impugning any and all advice backed by academic credentials. After all, that would include my own. I am saying that just because someone has a degree (or more than one) doesn't automatically mean his perspective is sounder or more valuable than yours. Advanced letters don't by themselves spell superior ideas.

Throughout this book, I will use *expert, specialist,* and *professional* interchangeably, not necessarily to indicate the quality of their counsel, but to recognize their commonly perceived authority.

Advice by dire prediction. Expert advice often includes a warning: Ignore this, and you risk the consequences, often unseen and far away.

For example, "Spank your child, and he will learn to solve problems through force, becoming more likely to abuse his own children." Or, "Set your standards too high, and your children will rebel against them when older." Or, "Insist that a teen attend church, and he will someday abandon religion."

When someone definitively predicts psychological peril in disregarding his words, you might want to question not only his predictions but also his words. Forecasting far down the road is marked by unforeseen curves and detours, especially if the road is travelled by young people. Too many miles of life can intervene.

Advice as a Resource, Not a "Rule"

However and from whomever it comes to you, advice can be useful or useless, helpful or harmful, moral or immoral. How, then, should we separate that which is to be accepted from that to be rejected?

Ask some questions. The most critical is this one: How does this advice mesh with my deepest held beliefs and morals? Whatever an expert proposes is often colored by her personal views. She may little value what you most value for your child's character.

To illustrate, computer search "self-esteem." The search results run into the tens of millions, as most experts rank self-esteem at or near the top of the personal well-being scale (though the research doesn't support this). Search "childhood humility" and compare the number of results. Humility is just not a select topic for most experts.

What if you consider humility a more desirable quality than overemphasized self-image? Are you psychologically unschooled? Or are you teaching your own values, independent of an expert's viewpoint? So much of "proper" parenting these days revolves around the misleading question: What is psychologically correct? The answer: In whose judgment?

Does the advice line up with your lived experience? Give it the squint test. If your reflective reaction to it is a half-closed, skeptical eye, your face may be telling your brain: Think this one over; don't take it at face value. If an idea sounds flaky, it just might be.

Does the advice square with common sense? You have a reservoir of knowledge about people and life. It's called by various names: instincts, intuition, judgment, horse sense, gut. Someone somewhere once observed that sound advice often evokes a forehead slap that says, "Of course, I knew that!"

One mother I know regularly relied on her belly test. If something sat uneasy in her belly and she didn't quite know why, she knew it needed more scrutiny. Her aim was to eventually put her gut sense into words. Then the kids would have something concrete to argue about.

The adage is: *It's an ill wind that blows no good.* Meaning, something has to be really bad to bring no benefit whatsoever to anyone. Some of the fifty "expert opinions" in this book may strike you as nonsense. Some may sound sensible until scrutinized more closely. Much advice is more or less a mix: It can work for some parents with some kids under some circumstances. It is not, however, a good guide for all, or even most, parents. Some advice is worth ignoring because it can cause more problems than it solves. It can mislead more than it leads.

"But Dr. Ray," you may rightly be asking, "isn't *Advice Worth Ignoring* itself a piece of advice?" Why, yes, it is. So you must judge for yourself: Does anything I say have merit for your family with your morals? Does it make sense? Does it align with wisdom confirmed through generations? If so, consider it. If not, ignore it.

Early Misdirection

The birth of a first child also births first-time insecurities. The pressure to start out right can be intense. After all, these are the formative years, aren't they? Couldn't mistakes made now reverberate beyond little Primo's first Social Security check?

Understandably, new parents lean heavily on guidance from others: Grandma, veteran parents, the professionals. Most everybody seems to know more than they do, or at least sounds like it. And sorting through it all can be a monologue in self-doubt.

"I heard yesterday on *30-Minute Mother* that laying a baby in his crib while he's still crying can create trust issues. But I've been walking with him for two hours. My legs are twitching, and I'm frustrated. And he has to sense that. Maybe he's hungry. No, I've fed him twice in the last hour, and the *Baby Diet Rite* book says that overfeeding can develop extra fat cells for life."

Young parenthood is marked by trial-and-error guesswork. Bad advice, however, can elevate normal uncertainty to groundless anxiety.

Idea #1: Personality Is Formed Early

"Personality is formed by age five or six." So the theory goes.

Looking back, I've changed quite a bit since kindergarten. Even well into first grade I had no political views, had weak morals, and would have found writing this book to be a real struggle, with the best of crayons. Admittedly, some of my youthful immaturity lingers, but overall my personality has been a work in progress for decades, as I suspect has yours.

This theory—call it the "personality finality" myth—was born in the youth of psychiatry. Its father was Freud, who declared that every child had to navigate several "psycho-sexual" stages, the most critical unfolding prior to age six. How well a child did so laid the groundwork for adult emotional health or struggles. Though most clinicians no longer think like Freud, the idea that personality is set very young remains stable in the cultural psyche.

• • •

During seminars, I ask parents, "How many of you have a child under age six?" Hands rise everywhere. I then order them, "Leave immediately, and go straight home. Your time to shape your child's personality is fading fast."

So far no one has ever left. I'd like to think they fear missing one sentence of my presentation. More likely, when so stated, my advice sounds pretty ignorable.

The truth is that temperament, or one's inborn nature, can indeed show itself quite young. Shy, fretful, aggressive, outgoing—all manner of traits have an internal wiring component, which can influence someone for better or worse throughout life.

Too, mistreatment in the womb or soon thereafter through substance abuse, malnutrition, or neglect can have reverberating ill-effects on the brain. On the other hand, the lifelong influence of loving, caring parents can go a long way toward reshaping the way a child thinks and behaves. And this kind of abuse and neglect is radically unlike the effects of the range of parenting choices that diligent, loving parents make during the course of their on-the-job-training. In other words, good moms and dads don't risk malforming their child's developing personality through their all-too-human ways.

My wife and I adopted all of our children. Our twins, whose earliest years were filled with neglect and chaos, came to us at age four. Had we believed we had at most a couple of years to reverse the trajectory of their lives, we would have panicked, fretful over just how to jam fifteen years of parenting into two. Where are the kids now? At age twenty-four, both are working and living independently. (Yes!) And like their parents, they are still maturing.

Christians believe that faith in Christ renews one's soul. The old person passes away, and however gradually, a new and better person is created. Is God so limited that if he doesn't reach someone prior to elementary school, he is too late? All conversions must happen young, or they pretty much won't happen? Nothing I've read has ever indicated any apostle first followed Jesus as a preschooler.

For most, parenting is a two- to three-decade phase of life, sometimes longer when the young adult trickles back home, setting up residence in the basement. Make one childrearing "mistake" per day—an over-reaction, misjudgment, inconsistency—and over twenty years the total tops seven thousand. For me, one a day is a good day. God made children resilient, able to withstand, thrive even, when raised by mistake-prone adults.

A fear of mistakes works against good parenting. You become unsure of yourself, second guessing your judgments, anxious about making a wrong move that will echo psychologically for years, culminating in your child becoming an afternoon TV talk-show guest—given a whole week of his own. Parents have plenty enough to worry about without old, false theories of personality unsettling them.

I once asked a group of women, "When is personality finally formed?"

One quipped, "When you're married?"

"No," I replied, "when your life is over."

"Same thing," she replied.

Tough crowd.

Idea #2: Children Are Naturally Cooperative

A college student asked me, "Do you think children by nature are cooperative?" In full psychologist mode, I answered with a question, "What do *you* think?"

She replied, "I think that children are more willful than cooperative, but my child-development professor thinks the opposite. He asked this question on our exam, and he's made it clear what answer he expects." *How uncooperative,* I thought.

If children are born predisposed to cooperate, then it follows that they shouldn't need all that much discipline. Most would be inclined to obey. Mom and Dad would only have to "facilitate appropriate behavior." Thus, more guidance, less discipline.

As we shall see throughout this book, this presupposition has spawned a range of highly questionable advice. Begin with an erroneous premise about human nature, and the ideas following from that premise will likewise be erroneous.

• • •

G.K. Chesterton, an author and clear-eyed social commentator, observed that the one Christian doctrine with abundant empirical proof is that of original sin. We are born bent toward the self.

What is among the earliest of toddler credos? "Mine!" No one has to teach it to her. It bursts from within. Does Mom have to counsel, "Remember, Charity, you don't need to share your toys. Keep them to yourself." Has any dad ever heard this from his son, upon sending him to the corner for punishment? "Don't forget, Father. Set the timer. And feel free to leave the room. No need to watch me." Yeah, right.

In a few pages we will scrutinize the so-called "terrible twos." Would they be called terrible if kids didn't do what comes naturally and assert more of their inborn selves? Terrible twos and being naturally cooperative, it would seem, are mutually contradictory.

Kids do vary widely in their inborn willfulness. At the easier end of the continuum are those inclined to get along with others, even parents. These Harmonys and Ernests are a minority, but they do exist. (I read about a family in Nova Scotia with three of them.)

An agreeable firstborn can make you cocky, feeding the attitude: "This is easy. I don't see any of the troubles other parents talk about. My daughter knew early on that my 'no' means 'no.' I was not about to hang my knickknacks from the ceiling in wire cages." Then comes child number two, who uses your knickknacks for target practice.

I've labeled this the "shell-shocked second child syndrome." Child number one is not normal. She is a freebie, a mulligan round from God: "Here, Mom, raise this for starters. The real kid is coming next."

Most parents know from experience that kids will challenge at least as much as they cooperate. Still, their descriptions convey otherwise:

"He is so strong-willed."

"She's quite the challenge."

"He is extremely high-maintenance."

"She is seven going on seventeen."

"We have a difficult child."

These descriptors merely reinforce the expectation that little Igor should be easier to raise, more cooperative. If not, then he must be strong-willed, high-maintenance, etc. On the other hand, if willful is more or less the norm, then strong-willed is more or less the norm. It would be more accurate to say, "normal-willed," or if you will, "child."

Am I playing with words? Does it matter how one describes a child's nature? Yes, in a number of ways.

First, it mischaracterizes the child. Chuckie is not in reality some little hellion who requires extraordinary effort to guide. Believing this can cause undue frustration and impatience in his parents. Put as a question: Who would seem harder to discipline, a child whose parent thinks of him as "normal," or one thought to be "abnormally tough"?

Second, overestimating the strength of a child's will can lead to pinball discipline, bouncing from approach to approach, searching vainly for something that will finally move this immoveable youngster.

"I tried using corner time for discipline, but after two weeks, nothing changed. So I started sending him to his room. He just lay on his bed and stared at the ceiling. Then I took away his favorite stuffed dog, but after an initial cry-fest, he didn't even ask about it anymore. Finally, I got so exasperated that I sent him next door to run an errand and moved the family while he was gone."

Pinball discipline teaches the child, "Will, keep resisting. I'll tire, relent, and look for something else." It teaches him to persevere beyond our discipline stamina. It creates the false impression that nothing works for this child. He eats consequences for lunch. Why can't he cooperate like other kids? Most likely, he can. The pinball discipline is what is stiffening his will, especially toward the people doing the pinballing.

Third, inconsistent, tentative, or permissive discipline can shape a child's nature into something much more unpleasant. It's a basic equation: Weak discipline equals stronger will. It is one thing to be willful. It is quite another to be willful and *defiant*.

On parents' first office visit, routinely I ask, "Do you think your child is strong-willed?" Nearly as routinely I hear, "Oh yes, without a doubt. He pushes and resists us constantly." After a few sessions improving discipline skills, I reask the question. Their answer surprises them, "It's like I'm living with a different child." Still childlike and willful, just no longer as oppositional.

In looking back, I wouldn't consider any of my own children particularly strong-willed. I know, you're probably thinking, this guy raised one child too many. His memory is fading. Actually, there's a better explanation: The strongest-willed of our children was not stronger-willed than his mother.

The key to living well is learning how to control and direct one's will. A little person isn't capable of doing this on his own. He needs help from big people. And most of the time those big people are parents, who for their child's sake must regularly assert their will over his.

IDEA #3: NEVER LET THEM "CRY IT OUT"

Little ones cry—lots. (Years of schooling give me these insights.) And with little or no language, they can't say why, leaving you to speculate. Fortunately, much of the time, it's the basics—thirst, hunger, fatigue, diaper dumps, clothing chafing (more common with girls).

Unfortunately, fixing the basics doesn't always fix the distress or lower the decibel level. Then what? As Bliss's upset rises, so can yours, sometimes to the point of shared tears. "What's the matter? What should I do now?... How fast can my mother get here?"

A parent who predictably answers a child's cries, be they physical or emotional, sends the soothing message: *I'm here for you.* And no doubt, a pattern of neglecting a child's distress does risk emotional trouble. The key word is *pattern,* neglect that is consistent, creating an emotional distance that pervades the relationship.

Our grandmothers, when they were young mothers, called the puzzling upset "being fussy." With little angst, they realized their limits and sometimes gave the child time to self-soothe. They weren't tormented by doubts about letting nature help them out.

Young mothers today don't have that peace. They've been warned: Crying conveys a need. The longer the cry, the deeper the need. Fail to meet that need, no matter how unclear it is, and the child will feel insecure, ignored even.

An expert on a radio program intones: "A parent must always and immediately respond to a baby or toddler's crying, or she can stunt the child's emotional growth. Well into adulthood the child may show blunted empathy for others, as she herself didn't receive proper empathy when very young."

Having tuned in to this program, I remember feeling a lot of empathy for the young parents listening, this despite that decades ago my own mother periodically let me cry myself to sleep, supposedly stunting my early capacity for empathy.

• • •

About age nine months, our daughter Hannah started to wail nonverbally that her crib was too confining, this at around three every morning. Some "child attachment" advocates would urge, "Go to Hannah. She obviously wants and needs you." My wife and I sleepily did so—sort of. Taking turns getting Hannah (I negotiated for a turn every sixth night), we carried her to a playpen (gasp!) in the family room, thus muting her rage to a distant rumble. After a few weeks, Hannah was sleeping peacefully through the night. She must have decided she didn't need us anymore—not at 3:00 A.M., anyway.

All of this is not intended to suggest that I recommend plopping your little one in bed—or as with Hannah, out of bed—whenever she's distraught and you're clueless as to why. How long you persevere in letting your little one cry is your call, and parents vary widely in their stamina, as do kids. I am advising, however, against being unnerved by the accusation that you are somehow a cold-hearted, unfeeling mom or dad if you don't persist in trying to soothe your child until mental or physical exhaustion, whichever arrives first.

It's worth repeating: *To sow the seeds for future personality flaws, neglect almost always has to build upon itself.* Typically it must be deliberate and indifferent. So rest easy. You needn't agonize that had you just endured for seventeen more minutes, your child would have been pacified, secure in his place in the world. Besides, how many "seventeen more minutes" had you already tallied?

IDEA #4: IT'S THE TERRIBLE TWOS

What is so "terrible" about being two? Is it because *no* emerges as the toddler's word of choice? Is it because a two-year-old operates at warp speed with no internal governor? Is it because trip-switch emotions can flare with the slightest trip? Is it because a two-year-old is mastering the look that says, "You're not the boss of me"?

Yes. However, for most parents, it is this last one that is the best measure of the adjective *terrible*.

A two-year-old is outgrowing the days of preferring to be in a parent's arms to anywhere else. He is heading out impetuously into the nearby world. He's on the move—places to go and people to see. His will is showing itself, along with an attitude that croons, "I did it my way."

Don't complain about your two-year-old to a parent of a teen, though. You could hear, "What's the problem? He spits out his peas? My kid wants purple hair with a nose ring. His school has my cell phone on speed dial." One mother observed, "Sixteen is the terrible twos times eight plus a driver's license."

Calling the twos "terrible" is a natural outgrowth of the more fundamental misconception that children are naturally cooperative. As such, once they start acting uncooperatively, they are acting "unnaturally," counter to what's to be expected. If, however, as I've argued, children are naturally willful—more or less, depending upon the child—the terrible twos is a misnomer. Better to say the typical twos.

The terrible twos may be typical, but it is not universal. Some kids get feisty in the twos, and some don't. And most still like their parents' arms. While some people might find these tots' babyish brattiness intolerable at times, at their size and intellect, they can only create so much turmoil.

In an "Ask the Expert" column, a mother wrote that her two-year-old wasn't the least bit terrible. In fact, he was a most pleasant little guy. Should she worry?

I expected an answer something like, "Count your blessings. Not all kids get tough in the twos." Instead, the doctor predicted that her "little angel" (his words) would soon change, and if not, yes, she should worry. He intoned that a child who behaves too well at that age often does so at the cost of his development and self-image.

Fast forward several years. What if Angelo is still angelic, at age ten, twelve, or even fifteen? Would mom feel compelled to seek a therapist, lamenting, "It all started in his twos. He was sweet then and still is. Is his self-image too far gone?"

Terrible twos implies a phase, a developmental thing. It comes with age and corrects itself with age. True, most kids do outgrow their two-year-old style, if Mom or Dad act to correct it. Otherwise, terrible twos could meld into the tantrum threes, the fiery fours, the fit-filled fives—well, you get the progression.

Counseling a parent of an unruly adolescent, I might ask, "When did all this begin?" Common answer, "When he was little." Unless a parent takes charge early on, little troubles in the twos can become big troubles in the teens.

My wife, Randi, has been a parent through seven two-year-olds. (I would have helped more, but I was busy writing parenting books.) We adopted three of our children after age two, so we missed our opportunity to act early. It was obvious to us that the adults present during those years missed it, too. Randi has always maintained, "The twos are relatively easy. The tricky stuff comes as they get older." Compared to disciplining a fourteen-year-old, disciplining a two-year-old is child's play.

Couple high energy level with low self-control, and a two-year-old can misbehave about every sixth breath. Still, discipline at that age is basic and straightforward: If you do A, I'll do B. As Discipline 101 says: *The earlier, the easier.*

So, do the terrible twos exist? Well, the twos do. As to *terrible*, that's a bad adjective. It mischaracterizes kids and misleads parents.

IDEA #5: IT'S A STAGE; IT WILL PASS

It may be a stage, but that doesn't mean it will pass. Even if it does pass, it's important to consider the "when." Will it pass on its own, with the passing of time? Or will it need some help from you to pass?

Childhood is marked by comings and goings of all sorts. Stages and phases of language, thinking, physical skills, hormones—all move in a somewhat predictable pattern. What about behavior? Does it flow upward and onward—from the immature to the mature, from the impulsive to the deliberate, from self-concern to concern for others?

Not surprisingly, misbehavior is also lumped into the stage concept, with some legitimacy. Particular ages are identified with the appearance of particular trouble spots. Two-year-olds can display newfound opposition. Six-year-olds can mutilate the truth once they realize that parents don't have eyes everywhere. Thirteen-year-olds can conclude that a parent knows little of life after forty years.

Parents confess, "He's never done anything like this before."

I ask, "How old is he?"

"Nine."

"Has he ever been nine before?" Meaning, new forms of misconduct show up with each age. As a rule, kids get smarter; and with smarter can come quicker and slicker.

• • •

The question is not: Do some behaviors follow age? They do. The more relevant question is: Will they pass? That all depends, mostly upon a key person—a parent. How a parent responds to the behavior in the main answers, "Will it pass?" If she believes it's natural to the age and takes a passive watch-and-wait posture, the "stage" may not pass. It may become a style. If she disciplines the stage, it should fade, sooner or later.

Unfortunately, a mother or father may tolerate tantrums from a three-year-old or disrespect from a teen because they've been reassured it's age-typical. It may be age-typical, but it's not age-good.

While the form of the unruliness may shift with time, the impulses driving it may not. A three-year-old's tantrum is pretty amorphous— lots of body torquing, limb flopping, leaking from facial orifices. A nine-year-old's is more targeted—nasty words, selective aggression, repeated arguments. A fourteen-year-old's can blend both ages and then some.

The eruption itself has morphed in shape, gone through stages, if you will. The underlying cause—uncontrolled emotions when thwarted—has not.

Whether a misbehavior is part of a stage or not is, for the most part, irrelevant to your parenting. The misbehavior is present. And whether it is present due to age or multiple other reasons, it still has to be addressed.

The good news: You probably did little to evoke this stage. It came in its time.

The bad news: You may have to do lots to discipline it. Otherwise, a stage can become a habit can become a pattern can become a personality.

Timely discipline can keep time-specific phases short.

Moral Questions

Shaping character is top priority for most parents. Love, affection, time, discipline—all are dedicated to raising a morally anchored young person.

The question naturally follows, "Are there ways to better do that?" Newer, more enlightened notions about moral upbringing have arisen to answer the question. Some blend truth with error. Some blend error with error.

IDEA #6: LIVE THE EXAMPLE AND CHILDREN WILL FOLLOW

Walk the talk. Show, don't tell. Values are caught, not taught—all variations of one theme: A good example is essential for good parenting.

No doubt, if you don't strive to live what you give, who knows what you'll get? Like heat-seeking missiles, kids lock in on inconsistencies and double standards. Rare is the parent who has never been accosted with, "Why do I have to if you don't?" or, "You tell me to show you respect, but you don't show it to me," or, "Maybe you should look at yourself." Owww.

Teaching by example forms a durable base from which to form character. It is the base, but alone it won't raise the kind of person you want. Being a moral adult is fundamental to teaching children morals. But it is not sufficient, in and of itself.

Parents tell me of their former belief that by being a model for their children, their children would follow. Talk nice to them, and they'll talk nice to you. Show generosity to a daughter, and she'll show it to her little sister. Keep the house clean, and a teen will keep his room clean.

Admirably, the adults tried hard to live up to their side of the equation. The kids didn't try nearly so hard to live up to their side. Is this a surprise? Children aren't typically moved by the same motives as parents.

Bluntly put, children are amateur and immature observers. In the short term, they aren't always attracted to even the best of examples. Only as they move beyond childhood do they come to fully appreciate and emulate their parents' ways. Much of good parenting doesn't make its mark until years later.

My children showed a bent for noticing my bad over my good. I could speak repeatedly with quality words like *muse* and *visage* and not once in passing did my kids try them out. Let one *damn* slip from my mouth, and cat-like quick they pounced, making my word theirs, temporarily anyway, until they got in trouble for talking like Dad.

In the youngest eyes, we are granted status worthy of copying. As the teenage years approach, we lose some of that. Merely because we old folks do it, it's not cool. An attitude forms: Not like Mom or Dad. Fortunately, most kids outgrow that attitude. Not because we get cooler with age, but because they get smarter with age.

I ask groups of parents, "Can you raise a child with a 'do as I say, not as I do' philosophy?"

"No," they all reply.

Then I suggest, "Of course you can. And we all do."

Let me qualify what sounds to be childrearing heresy. While living right makes for better parenting, none of us lives consistently right. Thus, we regularly must enforce standards we don't always meet. If you smoke, is it OK for your teen to smoke? Your language can get coarse; does that permit your ten-year-old the same self-expression? When you get frustrated, you can act like a five-year-old. Does that free your five-year-old to act like you when he gets frustrated?

A thirty-six-year-old mother came to me with several complaints about her twelve-year-old son: He watches too much television, he eats too much, and he's lazy. We explored why Mom had allowed these habits. Conclusion: "I watch too much television, I eat too much, and I'm lazy."

"Do you want your son to be like you?" I asked.

"Not in my bad habits," she said.

"Then you will have to set some limits and enforce them, even though your personal self-discipline in these areas has been lacking."

After twenty years of adulthood, Mom was still struggling to model mature behavior for her son, all the while believing she had little right to require better of him than she required for herself.

My hope is that my children reach beyond me in character. I don't want to be their moral ceiling. That makes me responsible to guide and discipline them in directions I don't always follow. And above all, to show them mercy for their human frailty, as I ask them to show me that same mercy for mine.

So the next time you hear something like, "You don't do that," don't let that be the final word. Respond, "You're right. I should, and I'm working on it. Besides, I want you to be better than me." That should make them mad.

Idea #7: Let Children Decide Their Morals

A television show once asked me to be a guest for the topic: Should parents force their values upon their children, or should they give them the freedom to choose for themselves? ("Force" versus "freedom." Doesn't take a shrink to analyze that show's bias.)

Had I accepted, I had several opening questions for the host. At what age does a child's moral freedom begin? Who decides right and wrong in the meantime? What if his morals hurt, even shatter, family peace? If the parents surrender their moral influence, who takes over—society, media, peers, pop culture?

Here's a childrearing experiment. As soon as Cookie is old enough to make personal decisions, do not require her do anything. Put your own values and wishes for her entirely on the shelf. Lima beans or Twinkies—her choice. Church or television—equal options. Hug her brother or smack him—whatever. She can share if she wants, refuse if she wants, visit her grandmother if she wants.

With each passing year, will she choose more good things and reject more bad ones? Do her actions grow more moral? Is she getting to be a smarter, more rational creature? Or will she immature into a self-absorbed, amoral young adult? Most parents, some kids, too, intuitively realize the picture wouldn't be pretty.

Some experts might not.

A popular parenting program advises parents not to tell children what is right or what is wrong when pursuing open communication. That's "moralizing," and it implies the child can't form his own morals. He can, but what would they look like?

The most open-minded parents liberally use force—not physical, but social and moral. When necessary, they make a child do what she resists and not do what she desires. Kids aren't naturally inclined toward everything that's in their best interest. (Who is?) If they were, how much parental "interference" would they need? The whole growing up process would be far less demanding.

In our feelings-rule culture, for an act to be "real," one must feel like doing it or want to do it. If not, its sincerity is questionable. If it is imposed from without, little settles within. The roots are shallow, easily pulled up.

This notion has transferred to morals. Teaching clear-cut rights and wrongs, in the name of "religion," is psychologically acceptable so long as a child remains open. Once she balks, though, instruction borders on compulsion. Living by such logic, passing on any values—moral or otherwise—would be linked to a child's willingness to cooperate. I'll confess, as a forward-looking third-grader, I felt no need to master the multiplication tables. Both my teacher and my parents made me. Talk about rigid compulsion.

• • •

Once upon a time, few if any questioned the need for one generation to pass morals on to the next. Not everyone agreed on what exactly should be passed on. But all agreed that the older had the duty and the experience to best do the job. Allowing children to sort through diverse moral options, choosing those that most suit them, would have been unthinkable. It wouldn't even have been debated.

The journalist Malcolm Muggeridge observed, "We have educated ourselves into imbecility." Entertaining the idea of self-taught morals, indeed putting it forth for serious discussion, seems a clear example of Muggeridge's assertion. It has the sound of educated enlightenment, but how real-world smart is it?

The proponents of giving a child his moral freedom would have to admit that it's most suitable to older children, the second half of childhood, if you will. Where does that leave the first half? No one would advise (at least no one I've ever heard) that parents take a passive, hands-off role, allowing young children to shape their own conscience. For one, they're not capable in any way—developmentally, intellectually, emotionally. For another, when they do approach the age of "reason," what would they have to build upon? What if previous bad choices lead to more bad choices in a sort of downward moral spiral? In other words, to form your own morals, you must have some kind of moral base from which to make judgments. Even were one given latitude to moralize himself, how handicapped would he be by his earlier decisions?

One might disagree with what a parent teaches—as I suspect lurked in the agenda of the TV show that called me. Nonetheless, parents have first right to teach it. Do some parents teach so badly that a child could do a better job? Yes. And fortunately, many children grow up to make more mature choices than their parents ever did.

Throughout my teen years, my mother insisted I visit my ninety-plus-year-old aunt, an activity near the bottom of my adolescent to-do list. Did she risk making me one day shun old people? I don't think she ever worried about that. Or did she "force" me to see a stage of life I needed to see and wouldn't look at on my own? Long after Mom was no longer my motivator, I kept visiting the elderly. Over time, I came to appreciate them more.

And as I move closer to that age group, I appreciate more my nieces and nephews who are forced to visit me.

IDEA #8: PUT YOUR STANDARDS TOO HIGH AND YOUR KIDS WILL REBEL

I attended a conference at which a therapist, whose specialty was adolescents, proclaimed authoritatively, "We all know that teens will rebel if a parent's standards are too high." Had I been feeling more rebellious, I would have spoken up: "No, we don't all know that, and all teens won't rebel." Call it my inner adolescence.

When the experts make statements like this, what kind of "standards" are they talking about? Academics, sports, music, chess, power lifting? In the pursuit of skills, parents can certainly push too hard, living through their child, substituting their own ego for their child's performance. Depending upon how hard they push, ignoring the signs of push-back, they could find themselves facing full-out rebellion, even shut-down.

Unfortunately, this advice isn't always limited to achievements or skills. All too often, it refers to the shaping of a child's character. The warning: Put your moral expectations too high, and your child will maneuver around or outright reject them as unreasonable and unreachable.

• • •

Yes, if a parent is dictatorial and unloving, he does risk raising a child who resists his standards. An unfeeling code of conduct can be seen as a "my way or the highway, kid" ruling style. The saying is, "Rules without relationship can breed rebellion."

A critical distinction must be drawn between strong parenting with love and strong parenting without love. Too often the caution is that no matter how loving you are, if you expect too much good behavior, you are asking for psychological trouble. Your high expectations will be the very thing to fuel your child's unruliness.

"High standards" is not an absolute phrase. It is relative to the situation. A standard can look extreme when compared to a slipping group standard. These days, morals are often measured by the norm. If it's normal, it's right. And yet, if the norm is unhealthy, then what is healthy is actually out of the norm, or as it were, abnormal.

Once upon a time, parents instinctively understood that enforcing high standards was their priority. The higher the standards, the better. It was the lack of standards—not their presence—that led to living a marginal existence. Only of late is the reverse proclaimed: Standards too far above the group norm can lead to living on the margins.

This advice finds face in the stereotype of the preacher's child, who as most everyone suspects is the sneakiest, most morally profligate kid in the congregation. Nodding yes to Dad's teaching, he says no to following it, flying under his parents' radar. What most everyone suspects, though, turns out to be more wrong than right. In reality, most preacher's kids grow up reflecting, not rejecting, their upbringing. According to one recent Barna study, pastor's kids are no more likely to walk away from the faith than other Christian teens. False ideas are sustained by the exceptions that do fit the stereotype.

"High standards risk rebellion" can keep you from resolutely taking stands that deep down you believe are right. After all, Dorothy already thinks she has the Wicked Witch of the East for a mother and Attila the Hun for a father. So you'll only make things worse by being "too controlling," the reigning accusation against parents who adhere to nonnegotiable principles. Compromising here and there will make your morals appear more doable.

How do you compromise standards you worry might be too high?

If you used to hold the line against dishonesty, for example, what would you say? "You should always be honest, Truman, but 'always' does seem a bit demanding, so how about a maximum of two lies a week, three if they're small."

Or if in the past you expected your children to get along, what would the new rule be? "Treat your sister with respect, Justice, but if you feel you can't, try not to curse at her, OK?"

What about the standards for dating? "We realize, Chastity, that our no-dating-until-seventeen rule is stricter than most other parents', so at age fourteen you can start romantic texting relationships." To compromise a standard, one has to allow exceptions to it. And it is the exceptions that weaken its spirit.

Of course, kids do push against rules and limits, as they neither fully understand nor appreciate them. Young minds routinely judge even the most reasonable expectations as unreasonable or unjust. It's in the youthful nature to survey peers' lives and challenge, "How can all their parents be wrong and you be right?" Indeed, regular comparisons are one sign that your standards are at a healthy high. Thank your kids for their vote of confidence.

Notice, though, they cite only those who "have it better." Never would Lulu breathe a word about Madge, who helps her mom all morning Saturday with housework, or about Ford, who is not allowed to drive until eighteen. Only when looking back through adult eyes, especially those magnified by raising their own children, do they realize how right Mom and Dad were.

A high standard is an ideal, a goal to strive for. It is not something kids or parents reach perfectly. It is not the standard that causes rebellion. It is the style in enforcing the standard.

On the other hand, your children are not walking a raised moral plane by themselves. You are walking with them. Everybody is raised well when the standards are elevated.

IDEA #9: IT'S NORMAL

Three-year-olds and temper fits are partners. Brothers battle—it's part of being brothers. What child doesn't get more lippy in the teen years?

All standard—normal?—analyses of kid conduct. Which begs the question: What is "normal"? Does it mean average, as in "a 100 IQ is normal"? Does it mean typical, as in "seventy-seven out of one hundred fifteen-year-old boys' rooms resemble a landfill"? Does it mean predictable, as in "occurring in most cases"?

What we mean by normal (a better term might be "age-normal") is clearer when talking about a child's development—motor coordination, speech, intellect, height, hormones. These lend themselves to patterns, following a somewhat expected age and stage progression. On the other hand, much oppositional or unruly behavior waxes and wanes throughout childhood, not necessarily following a predictable path. When talking about conduct, the boundary of "normal" is much fuzzier.

For our purposes, let's define normal as "typical," as in "behavior or patterns seemingly common to a particular age or stage." That is what most people mean when they observe, "It's normal."

• • •

For most parents, the critical question to consider is not, "Is it normal?" The critical question is, "Is it good or right?" Much that is normal is not desirable.

Mutual name-calling may be standard for many, if not most, siblings. It's not good. Massaging the truth may be the default option for seven-year-olds upon realizing that Mom is not omniscient. It's not right.

Normal has become a new measure for gauging what is acceptable. It is routinely followed by the unspoken, "Expect it. That's what most kids do." It is one thing to expect it; it is another to accept it.

"It's normal" has some appeal as a mark of behavior. It can be a sign of psychological OK-ness. It can imply a youngster is not socially odd or "disordered." It's reassuring to hear that your kid is acting like other kids, and that he's not off the behavior charts. With good behavior, we want our kids to be in the extreme. With bad, in the middle.

"It's normal" soothes a parent's self-image. It affirms that Mom or Dad aren't to blame for this brand of trouble. They haven't failed and aren't bad parents. Better to say, "It's normal," even if it's bad, rather than "I'm not a good parent."

Whether a behavior is normal or not is for the most part irrelevant to your parenting. It is happening, and you may have to address it. Whether Rocky punches Bruno once every seven weeks or seven times a week, Bruno is still being punched and Rocky is still being punchy. The former frequency is typical; the latter is atypical. No matter, each needs to be managed or disciplined.

Iris's eyes reflexively roll toward the ceiling any time you offer some opinion. Your survey of your friends indicates Iris pretty much sees things the way their teens do. What does that mean in your home? Not much. Eye rolling is demeaning, whether done less often than others do it, the same, or lots more.

The question, "Is it right?" and its partner, "Do I need to do something about it?" are far better guides for raising a morally mature youngster than, "Is it normal?"

Idea #10: Avoid Value-Laden Words—They're Bad

In graduate school, I was taught a second language. Call it the language of non-judgmentalism. It speaks like this:

"Angela, pushing Conan is *unacceptable.*"

"Don't you think that jumping on my desk is *an unfortunate decision,* Cliff?"

"We don't ride our bike through the flowers, Harley. *It's inappropriate.*" (What's with *we*? It's been decades since I've ridden my bike through the flowers.)

Politicians, too, have adopted the lexicon. Not, "I was wrong," but, "Mistakes were made."

This fashionable lingo has replaced older, outdated or guilt-inducing conventions like *wrong* and *bad.* In this day and age, according to the experts, no child should *ever* be talked into feeling guilty.

Using morally neutral words, it follows, is a good way to avoid moral judgments. "Unacceptable" or "inappropriate" sends no moral message. Instead it says, "Don't do that here, at this time." The context of the behavior is what makes it unacceptable. Not so much the action itself.

• • •

Let's take another look at that. Is any behavior actually wrong? Kicking the dog? Biting your sister? Rooting for the New York Yankees (if you live in Boston)? From a moral perspective, is it wrong to call some behavior "bad"? Is a husband who selfishly abandons his wife and three children "acting inappropriately"? Or is he wrong, *very wrong* and his actions bad, *really bad?*

By making a distinction between what a child does and who he is, parents attempt to avoid inducing needless guilt (or its cousin, shame) while attempting at the same time to instill positive feelings in a child despite his negative behavior.

"You are good, but your behavior is not."

"I like you—*I don't like what you did."*

"Your conduct is unpleasant—you're not."

Though their efforts are well intended, such distinctions are all too often lost on the child. Children, particularly younger children, can't easily separate actions from self. This is why little Justice thinks he's not a good person after he misbehaves. His instinctive, elementary conclusion is: "I acted bad, so I am bad."

To differentiate "who I am" from "what I do" is the kind of sophisticated thinking that evolves over years. The smartest of philosophers have debated how one's behavior and self-image or identity mesh.

How then does a child conclude she is loveable even when her behavior is not? By being loved—through warmth, affection, attention, time, and discipline. To develop a deep-seated sense of unworthiness, a child has to live with the relentless message that she is unworthy. Identifying a piece of conduct as what it is—bad or wrong—doesn't negate a parent's countless other expressions of love.

It is a gross overinterpretation to assert that labeling misconduct with any language other than nonjudgmental words causes a child to question his own value. If centuries of experience are any guide, it is not the presence of moral words that causes psychological trouble. Rather, it is the absence of them.

Calling lying, cheating, stealing, and screaming at one's mother "unacceptable" or "impermissible" trivializes their moral status. Socializing a child involves teaching her how to do less bad and more good. Some experts might be averse to using those terms, but most parents aren't. And they are the ones who decide what is good for their child and family.

IDEA #11: DON'T HAVE TOO MANY CHILDREN

Few experts make this statement so bluntly, though many insinuate it. Surprisingly, it is other parents—often family members—who are so blunt. In our culture today, there are just three things that most people object to across the board: smoking, spanking, and having more than 2.21 children. (OK, my tongue is planted in my cheek, but not firmly.)

Many people react to such "high-profile sins" by asking "clever" questions to make their point—questions that, in fact, quickly become both predictable and tiresome:

"Are they all yours?"

"Don't you have a TV?"

"So this is it, right?" (Usually follows child number two, almost always after number three.)

"You've got your boy and girl" (the "complete" family), *"so...are you finished?"*

Sometimes the intrusive queries come with an edge:

"Do you know what's causing this?"

"I hope you're done. How can you give each the attention it needs?" (It?)

"How are you going to afford sending them all to college?" (The financial lurks beneath many comments.)

There is risk to verbally cornering veteran mothers. These are ladies forged in the trenches with multiple little humans. They can swat away a rude remark as effortlessly as a seven-year-old's tattle.

"Is this all your family?"—Of course not, the oldest is at home with the triplets.

"Do you know what causes this?"—No, please tell me.

"Are you having any more?"—Well, not right this minute.

"Don't you think you might have too many children?"—Which one should I give back?

Upon hearing, "I'm sure glad it's you and not me," without pause one mother responded, "With that attitude, I'm sure my kids think so, too."

. . .

A grand irony in all this rests in our society's intolerant demand for tolerance. Tolerance is reserved for those who think correctly, as defined by reigning social mores. One "moral" edict to be accepted is sexual freedom, except, that is, the sexual freedom to have babies in marriage.

A father of ten told me that after child number five, he kept to himself news of his wife's pregnancies, as he simply didn't want to hear the refrains of negative remarks. Out-of-state relatives would just have to be shocked at his family's growth at the next holiday to come around.

When my wife and I trouped through a public place with our ten children, we were a spectacle. It might have been because of the shepherding dog we always had with us. Because of the various skin colors of the kids, though, we didn't hear much critique. Adoption lends a certain allowance to family size.

Why in a few short decades have larger families become such a target? After all, some of those who question pregnant moms themselves grew up in a generation where several children per family was not atypical. And they look back fondly on their own family life.

A few justify their criticisms out of "concern for the earth." Meaning, it's OK to criticize any family that is breathing in more than its fair share of oxygen and gobbling up a disproportionate amount of the world's resources. This one isn't so much on the minds of friends and family members. Their observations are more everyday and personal.

Some claim to be concerned for Mom's welfare: *I just worry about your taking on too much. How is your stress level? Are things OK?* However well-meaning, such comments imply that Mother doesn't quite understand the multiplying demands. With each child isn't she sacrificing more of herself? Well, yes she is. That's her intent.

Many objections are grounded in the material: *"How can you care for them?"* (Meaning what? Food? Shelter? Education? Cars? Bathrooms? Bedrooms?) And yet, the reality is that there has never been a time when, as a society, we have enjoyed such abundance.

The typical house not long ago was around one thousand square feet—one bathroom, two or more kids per bedroom, no air conditioning, one phone, single-car garage. Those who successfully raised families in such "deprivation" (though few called it that) now wonder how their own children can raise a four-child family in a house twice or more times as large, with more of everything.

During our adoption screening for our fourth child, the social worker asked, "Do you have sufficient bedrooms?" I was just about to answer, "Well, they do have walls, beds, and carpet. No TV though," until my wife's eyes closed my mouth. At the time, we had three bedrooms, seemingly sufficient to me. As plan B, Randi and I could sleep on the couch. OK, maybe I could.

When my oldest daughter, Hannah, entered college, at orientation the school's president talked with the freshmen about adjusting to a roommate. At which Hannah exclaimed, "Only one?" She had entered dormitory heaven.

I am not aware of any studies anywhere that conclude that being part of a multi-child family has any kind of psychologically stunting effects on the children (or for that matter, on the parents). In fact, in talking with now-grown multi-sibling children, the sense is overwhelming: They loved growing up in a big family.

Understandably, a parent may wonder, "How can I give each child enough individual attention?" I started to wrestle with this right around child number four. To which my wife observed—she should write my books—"Ray, they have brothers and sisters." In fact, I did notice a lot of the time they preferred to play with each other over me, as I whined,

"Hey, you guys, I used to be able to run fast. I don't want to always have to be steady pitcher."

The best answers are the softer ones: We've always been grateful for more kids; love multiplies—it doesn't divide. Sometimes a good response is no response—a smile, shrug, blank look. All of these say, "I don't understand your point."

What wins over naysayers most is the children themselves. Parents of a bunch typically invest heavily in their families. In time, others will see not emotionally and materially shortchanged young people, but ones who are maturing well. And who are admired by the very people who once didn't understand you.

Discipline Don'ts

Some discipline practices have been around as long as there have been parents and kids. Others have been around at least for many generations. These practices have been basics of childrearing. Seldom were they questioned.

Of late these practices have been accused of being at the least questionable, at the worst psychologically harmful. Could so many parents in so many times and places have gotten it so wrong? How did so many "dos" of discipline become "don'ts"?

IDEA #12: DON'T TELL A TODDLER NO

"*Little kids are whirlwinds of motion.*" Agreed.

"*Little kids are hyper-fascinated by their immediate world.*" Sure.

"*Little kids make the curiosity of cats look like apathy.*" Absolutely.

"*Little kids who hear no are stifled.*" Disagree, with a vehement "No!"

What might a savvy parent say instead of no?

"Excuse me, Butkus, I'm not comfortable with your using the television screen for Kung Fu practice. I'm sensing a lot of aggression. Please kick elsewhere, or I might take five points from your token system. I'll add them back after the TV repairman leaves." (Note my liberal use of I-messages.)

What makes *no* such a no-no? Supposedly, it squelches a child's natural impulse to experiment with his world. It is inhibiting and controlling. It is just not an encouraging word. Same for its cousins: *don't* and *stop*.

Much preferred are more positive alternatives, like giving choices and redirection. "Isn't it better to punch the couch than your brother, Rocky? It's softer." Or, "Here's a ball, Hunter. It's more fun to throw than the hamster." The aim is to nudge Hunter into more acceptable pursuits, not to stop his pursuits altogether.

This does not apply only to little kids. A popular school discipline program instructs teachers to avoiding listing class rules in the negative. They are to be phrased in the positive. Instead of, "No talking out," it's "Raise hand to speak." Rather than, "No pushing or hitting," substitute "Keep hands and feet to self." Not, "No saying no," but, "Stay positive." (OK, I've not yet seen this last one.)

Picture the scenario. A state trooper is chastising you for doing sixty-seven miles per hour in a fifty-five- mile-per-hour zone. Would it be smart to correct him, "Officer, please stay positive. I would prefer you say, 'Stay within the posted speed limit' instead of 'No speeding.' You'd sound much less authoritarian, and I'd be more likely to comply"?

My hunch is the trooper sees no problem with his language, and you would quickly speed from a warning to a ticket.

• • •

Good childhood discipline parallels the adult world. Its landings are softer, but its goal is the same: to teach about life. And like it or not, life is riddled with *nos*, some quite disagreeable but nevertheless beneficial. *No* is an unalterable aspect of how the world operates, for big and little people.

A well-timed *no,* rather than restricting a child's freedom, actually broadens it. It tells Freeman clearly what not to do, for his sake and others'. "How about this instead?" doesn't teach Freeman about limits or self-control. It attempts to persuade him, in a supposedly nicer-sounding way, to choose to do something else somewhere else. It's based on the hope that he will willingly alter his desires to match ours.

Even the word *no* doesn't impede a child for long. Shadow a toddler, and within three minutes you'll observe that *no* has about the same impact as a ping pong ball hitting the hull of an aircraft carrier. Flash might slow for a nanosecond, just to find the face attached to that annoying word, before speeding ahead.

As our straight-talking trooper demonstrates, *no* doesn't carry much weight unless it's backed by consequences, be it a ticket or a time-out. Anyone deeply concerned with the adverse effects of *no* should likewise assert, "no discipline." It is the discipline that puts the damper on a child, not the word.

Good parenthood is a blend of yes and no. Knowing when to say no and enforce it leads to more yeses. *No* doesn't shrink a child's world; it expands it.

IDEA #13: DON'T DELAY DISCIPLINE

Does the name Pavlov ring a bell? He was the Russian scientist who trained dogs to salivate at the sound of a bell. The bell rang, food immediately followed, until (after a number of close pairings) the bell alone caused the dog's mouth to water. Pavlov also found that the optimum time between bell and food was a mere half-second. The longer the delay, the less saliva. The connection dried up.

Dog trainers know that, to teach, their response to a dog's behavior—positive or negative—has to be immediate. Otherwise, learning is muzzled. Duke isn't capable of reasoning, "Let's see. Ten minutes ago I urinated in the yard like the guy wanted me to. I should have gotten a treat by now." Dogs don't have, and never will have, the brain power to relate their conduct to consequences too far removed.

Little children are not dogs. For one thing, dogs listen better. For another, they are easier to potty train. There is, however, a discipline similarity. A very young child, though far smarter than a dog (maybe not Lassie), can't link his behavior to your discipline if much time has elapsed between the two. Sixteen-month-old Angel, who disturbed four whole church pews behind her, won't have a clue that's the reason she's being made to sit on the steps forty-two minutes later at home. Logistics permitting, Angel's disruption at church has to be managed at church.

Twenty-month-old Knap, who rages at bedtime, probably won't associate his tirade with losing his favorite breakfast, Fruity Dinosaur Flakes, the next morning. The time lag is too long, even if Knap was unconscious for most of it.

Discipline similarities between little kids and dogs disappear rapidly with age, however. Dogs, no matter how old, can never mentally grasp delayed discipline. Little kids can within a few years after birth. The typical three-year-old, and many two-year-olds, can benefit from postponed discipline, given a reminder. "You were mean to Grandma, Joy, so now you can't watch TV," even if that reminder comes after a half hour of struggling to convince Grandma that Joy really is a sweet child.

"Discipline immediately" has confused parents with older kids, too. A mother wonders whether to act on something she just learned her five-year-old did two days ago. A father only today hears of his nine-year-old's disrespect last week toward the neighbor lady, and thinks, "What can I do about it now?" The passage of time doesn't erode the value of discipline. Statutes of limitations make for good law, not necessarily good parenting.

• • •

Reality dictates that much, if not most, discipline has to be enforced later rather than sooner, for several reasons.

First, misbehavior often doesn't come to light until sometime after the fact. Well before first grade, most kids realize, "Hey, these big people aren't everywhere and don't know everything." As a result, more misconduct gets covert. We can't immediately discipline what we aren't aware of. Only if and when we do become aware can we act upon what we know.

Second, kids escalate. Upset at being disciplined, they pile one piece of misbehavior on top of another. Which ones do you discipline when? You need time to think and sort out your options. Let's say that Dusty and Misty are engaged in a post-tooth-brushing spit fight. When you arrive on the scene, they begin to push each other, argue with you, and get in one last spit, while kicking a bedroom door shut. Time becomes your ally. "Both of you are in bed now. I'll know by tomorrow what I'm going to do about all this." For a change, let the kids wonder what you're up to.

Third, children are innately capable of completely unexpected, boneheaded stunts. Stanford promises to spend the afternoon at the library with Webster. Two days later you find out differently. Instead Snake's mom took the boys and her son to the Felons in Chains concert. Stunned, you need time to digest this. You want to consult with your spouse, Snake's mom, Snake's probation officer, and a couple of parenting books. Better discipline comes with knowing the facts. And sometimes the facts only come out slowly.

Fourth, at peak emotions, discipline can get impulsive or harsh. Act the instant after hearing from Snake's mom, and you could roar into Stanford's room, firing off, "Unbelievable! You lied and you planned to lie all along. You went straight to the Fellas in Jeans concert, or whoever they are. As of today you are grounded until you're married!" Putting time between offense and discipline can make for calmer discipline. It avoids the unwanted clutter of ugly words. You never have to apologize for what you didn't say.

Let's assume, however, that your three-year-old doesn't quite grasp why he's being disciplined now for what he did then.

Returning to dogs, the smartest of them doesn't "understand" discipline. All they "know" is that their A leads to your B. Even when a child doesn't yet comprehend the purpose of discipline, he can still learn something from it. And some learning is better than no learning.

Discipline is seldom perfect, either in its effect or its timing.

Idea #14: Don't Make Your Child Fear You

Some years ago a child development professional and I were guests on a television show about spanking. The host asked me if I ever spanked my children. "Sure," I freely admitted, "some a little, some more, others never, depending upon the child and age." After my pithy sound bite, my fellow guest practically smacked me with her own sound bite, "Then your children fear you!"

I don't think so, but right now I fear you. Take a couple of deep breaths and chill. OK, I thought that, but didn't say it. What I did say was, "How can you say that? You don't know me or my children." Then I really stunned her. "Besides, I want my children to fear me, if that means a healthy fear of proper discipline. And since my wife and I are the ones who discipline, every so often their fear might become temporarily attached to us. As they mature, they'll come to understand the love behind our actions." I could have added but didn't, "And someday they'll be teenagers who (like most teens) fear no one and nothing."

My logic didn't budge her. In her view, arousing fear in any child at any time was a bad thing. Period.

The no-fear parenting philosophy has arisen in part through a redefining of *fear*. Not so long ago, the word could mean "respect." In itself, it was not a negative term. Modern childrearing lingo, however, has lumped it with other words that, once upon a time, were associated with healthy moral development, words like *guilt, punishment,* and *control.* Now all these terms have been tarred with a broad psychological brush.

If my co-guest had been using fear to mean "healthy respect," I would have answered her, "I totally agree with you. I'm trying to teach that kind of fear." That was not what she meant. She was convinced that were I to spank, reflexively my kids would cower, as though I, the grizzly, were just looking for reasons to swat my cubs.

• • •

For argument's sake, let's define fear as the specialist did—an unpleasant emotional reaction. Even so, much depends upon the context of the fear. I have friends who are police officers and judges. I don't fear them— under most circumstances, that is. Were they to arrest me or sentence me for a crime, then, friends or no, I would definitely fear them. Again, it's more accurate to say I would fear my circumstances.

Similarly, my father was a committed family man whose discipline was like so many fathers of his generation—no nonsense. Did I fear him? More accurately, I can say I feared his reaction were I to be caught in some transgression. I knew how much Pop loved me, and I also knew he would act with firmness if I crossed the line. It was that knowledge—call it fear if you want—that kept me in line.

My sister and I once were at the supper table, scrapping like we often did. My dad, sitting across from us, started to reach toward us. Instinctively, I flinched until I realized he was reaching for the salt, not me. Everybody laughed. I didn't put much meaning to it, and neither did my father.

Imagine my reaction, then, when my wife and my son Andrew, about age five at the time, were watching the "spanking" television show. Turning to him, Randi asked, "Andrew, are you ever afraid of Daddy?" Incredulously, he answered, "No way!"

I think that bothered me more than any of the specialist's criticisms.

Idea #15: Don't Discipline When You're Angry

Anger and inconsistency are a symbiotic duo: They feed each other. Anger in a parent can lead to erratic discipline, and erratic discipline promotes anger and frustration. Good parents work hard to discipline with a level head. The best parents though, even after many years or many kids, are still working on the level-headed part.

Everything considered, calmer discipline is better discipline. You don't lose credibility, you don't make personal attacks (for which you later need to apologize), and you don't overdo, grounding Noelle until next Christmas for something she did on Labor Day.

That said, "don't discipline when angry" is not a hard-and-fast admonition. Human beings—all human beings—have emotions, and emotions can take a while to cool. If you wait to discipline Noelle until your temper drops to room temperature, the situation could go unresolved until next Thanksgiving.

. . .

Discipline frustrations erupt for several reasons. The first is *self-investment*. We dedicate ourselves to our children's personal and moral well-being. When they don't cooperate and are seemingly meandering erratically toward maturity, a parent's self-doubt creeps in. *What's wrong? Is it me? Why isn't he getting this? Am I failing as a parent?* Such doubts, even if groundless, fuel overreaction. In my mind, Ripley's lying isn't about childish misconduct; it's about *my* inadequacy. Staying cool helps to avoid overthinking this.

Second, consider *emotional proximity*. It's a social law: Those closest to us can rile us most. And the parent-child bond is among the closest of those connections. On one hand, we love our kids with a strength unimagined pre-parenthood. On the other hand, they can so agitate us that anyone listening to our interchange would wonder which one is the child. Parents ruefully confess to talking meaner to their kids than to anyone else. (If they spoke like that to any adult, their kids would be the only ones left willing to talk to them.)

Third, for most of us *consistent, effective discipline is a last resort*, not a first course of action. Discipline is love, but it's not the kind of love most parents want to show. Thus, we'd prefer to rely upon words to get Conan to cooperate. We reason, persuade, negotiate, re-remind, add decibels, use add-ons like, "I mean it!", "Now!", or my mom's favorite, "I'm not talking just to hear myself talk!"

Because kids, by many measures, are not reasonable creatures, they can argue, ignore, challenge, and/or defy our most reasonable efforts. At some point, hitting our limit, we've "had enough!" Then we discipline.

Our high heat is what pushes us to act rather than the misconduct itself.

Even when the approach is fiery, the discipline may still be legitimate. After I subject Rocky to a twenty-minute harangue for smacking his brother, I send him to his room. The words may be excessive; room time isn't.

Anger can be discipline's ally. Proper anger can convey: *What you did was very wrong, and my emotion dramatizes that.* As a boy, I could gauge the gravity of my offense by Mom's or Dad's reaction. Not that I necessarily agreed with it, but it did make more obvious how they saw things.

When your temper causes you to overreact, what then? It's simple, though not always easy: Apologize, sooner or later—for the overreaction, not the discipline. An apology does not signal inconsistency or weak authority. It signals humility and confidence. It admits, "I was wrong in the way I handled things; I was not wrong for handling them." Of course, upon further reflection, you may have to apologize for the handling, too.

Calm is not always doable, not as long as parents and kids are human. Wait until you're absolutely self-composed to discipline, and you could wait too long. You no longer can recall what Buck did and why you were so mad about it. Discipline is sometimes a mix of good teaching and bad style. Later regrets over style? Again, say you're sorry, for your style, not for being a parent.

IDEA #16: DON'T DO "DOUBLE JEOPARDY"

At age four, my son Andrew attended preschool. His classroom had a number of play stations: blocks, corn kernels, sand, mechanical bull riding (just kidding—that was in the kindergarten class). One day, while digging in the corn kernels alongside another boy, Andrew abruptly flung a handful, some of which plastered his playmate. Why?

Who knows? As discipline, he was escorted from the corn box to the sand box. Brutal.

After school, his teacher summarized the incident for me and in so many words cautioned: *It's handled. No more needs to be done.*

On the drive home, I asked Andrew for his take. "Well, Dad, I know some things are good to do and some things are bad to do, but how can I know which is which until I try them all?" That did have a sort of childlike logic to it. Nevertheless, according to my grown-up logic, Andrew needed to learn which was which without having to try them all. Otherwise, it would be one long year.

That afternoon, Andrew spent some time in the corner and lost an afternoon of watching *Mister Rogers*. It was the one where they showed how they put makeup on the Incredible Hulk, too.

The next day I told the teacher of our response to the corn-kernel caper. Bothered, she replied, "That sounds like my grandfather: 'You get in trouble at school, you'll get in more trouble at home.'" Apparently, that meant our discipline was not only unnecessary, but overdone. She felt that the incident needn't concern us. It was handled among her, Andrew, and the other boy.

A kernel of truth, perhaps, but our thinking was that Andrew broke two rules. His teacher's ("Don't throw the corn") and ours ("Obey your class rules, so your teacher doesn't have to discipline you"). I don't know that Andrew's teacher agreed with my reasoning—for sure, Andrew didn't—but my wife did. We both believed we were the primary ones to teach Andrew, by added discipline if need be, to respect others' legitimate authority. If that's double jeopardy, we plead guilty.

• • •

In law, *double jeopardy* means that a person can't be tried a second time for the same offense, once he's been judged not guilty. Similarly, some education experts claim that a child shouldn't be disciplined a second time for an offense for which he's already been disciplined.

I have two problems with that: One, if Oliver Wendell is guilty of an initial offense, he isn't being unfairly retried. Two, if in the parent's judgment more response is called for, that parent is the court of final appeal.

One mother expressed to me her frustration over her adolescent son's Sunday school experience. His teacher, a volunteer, had contacted her repeatedly about his classroom behavior. Mom contended that her son was not the only disruption, that the teacher was a weak disciplinarian, and that her son would behave better if the teacher managed her classroom better. What's more, the mother questioned why she should discipline her son for something that she didn't witness, and for which she didn't have all the facts. (The teacher had addressed this issue by inviting her to sit with her son in class—something the mother was resistant to.)

I asked Mom, "Do you want your son to behave well only for those who are able to manage him?"

"Of course not."

"Then you'll have to manage him at home, regardless of how his teacher handles the class."

A strong sign of character is how a child treats others, whether they are strong or weak, firm or permissive, likable or not. When a child takes advantage of certain adults, it falls on the parent to supplement what these adults might lack in discipline skills or authority.

"Wait until your father gets home." Another something said back in our grandparents' day but said less today, for a number of reasons. One, there are fewer families in which Dad comes home at night. Two, there are fewer moms at home to make the threat. Three, fewer experts agree with this approach. To them, it rings of an unfair off-loading of authority onto a parent absent during the trouble.

Certainly a parent needs his or her own authority. And most daily disorder is better handled on the spot. But "I've got your back" is healthy support. Good marriages are a partnership. Each spouse adds to the other's strengths and strengthens the other's weaknesses.

My wife, Randi, is a stay-at-home mom. Through sheer numbers alone, on some days the kids could easily tag-team and overwhelm her discipline. Knowing that after answering to Mom, they may also later have to answer to Dad put the brakes on their bedlam. If, for example, I came home and found out that Randi had to confine a child to the corner several times, depending upon the account—Randi's, not the child's—I might add my own consequences: an earlier bedtime, extra chores, head-down-at-the-table time-out.

Our thinking parallels the explanation we gave to Andrew's preschool teacher: Two rules were broken. Mom's, which said, "Obey Mom." And Dad's, which said, "Don't give Mom a bad time." The message was: Mom and I are linked. Rattle her, and you rattle me.

Did this cast me as the enforcer? Did it tarnish my father image with the kids? Not that I could tell. One, the discipline wasn't personal or vengeful. It was a given of family operation. And two, the main offender varied daily, so no one child consistently felt picked on or could accuse us of "double jeopardy."

Besides, even if the kids temporarily viewed me as a bad guy, my wife viewed me as a good guy. More than an even trade-off.

IDEA #17: DON'T GIVE TIME-OUTS

In an article on time-outs, one professor quoted the National Association for the Education of Young Children, which denounced time-outs as "emotionally harmful," right up there with spanking or shaming. I thought: Don't sugarcoat it. Tell parents what you really think.

Hers is not the extreme sentiment of some academician somewhere. Many child-development folks concur. They regard time-out as ineffective, or worse, oppressive. Time-out has been tagged as socially isolating, emotionally insensitive, self-image bruising, and shame producing. Quite an indictment, if it were true.

Some experts see time-out as unreasonable because they see children as reasonable creatures who are eager to cooperate and can be guided with the right words and gentle persuasion. According to this "expert" view, time-outs short-circuit the person-to-person connection, effectively halting discussion and with it resolution.

Time-out is really shorthand. Its full, formal name is "time out from reinforcement." It emerged from the theories of behavioral psychologists, who proposed that behavior is moved primarily by the seeking of positives called *reinforcers*. What exactly is prompting or sustaining a behavior can be hard to pinpoint. So, time out from reinforcement eliminates all possible reinforcers by removing someone, usually a little someone, from the scene of his behavior.

Even among its advocates, many are quick to emphasize that time-out is not punishment. While punishment uses negatives, time-outs involve the temporary suspension of positives. Even as a rookie graduate student, I thought this a distinction without a difference. If a loss of freedom of movement is not a punishment, what is it?

• • •

Ask any child, "Do you like being forced to stay in one place while everybody around you can move where they want?" Would any child propose to his mother, "Do you mind if I spend a little quiet time in the corner? I think the meditation will do me good"?

Whether or not time-out is punishment isn't of concern to most parents. They rely upon it as a first-line, benign form of discipline, especially for younger kids. (For older ones, banishment to one's room and grounding are variants.)

Time-out may be momentarily unpleasant, but unpleasant does not mean unhealthy. Because a child doesn't like something doesn't mean it's not good for him. Think green beans. Like any discipline, time-out can be misused or corrupted. Locking a child in a closet for two hours isn't extreme time-out. It is abuse.

There are lots of good reasons to use time-outs, though. *First, it's easy and immediate.* Little kids can misbehave faster than we can think of consequences. Therefore, we need discipline that is right at our fingertips. Time-out is as simple as it gets. It is Discipline 101.

Unruly Conan is sent to a boring place—corner, chair, steps, couch—until he settles or his time is served. No need to instantly identify what privilege to curtail, or for how long. No need for his parent to think "What do I do now?" No need to decide how many stickers to remove from the reward chart. (My informal research has established that the average lifespan of a sticker system is 23.6 days or 96 stickers, whichever comes first.)

Second, time-out is portable. My preference is the corner. Few places are as dull as the intersection of two walls. Sit Nielson on a chair or steps, and he can still bide time watching the world go by. Corners also are everywhere, which is good for larger families. Most rooms come with a minimum of four. Fill those, and another room is mere feet away. When our ten kids were all aged twelve and under, our corners got backlogged, forcing us to delay sentences. "Show up in the family room next Wednesday at 7:00 PM. You have corner time."

Third, time-out is repeatable. You can use it once a day, once an hour, or once a minute. One expert warned that if a parent uses time-out more than a couple of times a day, something is wrong. He meant with the parent. But maybe the parent is just being consistent.

Fourth, time-out is flexible. Time can be adjusted depending upon the infraction, level of cooperation, or amount of snot smeared upon the wall. It can revolve around family schedule, a parent's need for peace, and a child's age. What about the "one minute per year of age" rule? That's an upcoming piece of advice worth ignoring.

As a psychologist for nearly forty years, I have yet to see one adult scarred by being timed out way back when. I have seen plenty who would have benefited from much more time in time-out.

Idea #18: Don't Force Manners

Want your child to make a great first impression, making you look like God's gift to parenthood? Require politeness—the first step of which is manners:

Please. Thank you. I'm sorry. Excuse me. These seven elementary words have social returns well beyond the effort needed to use them. When our children were young, my wife and I introduced a family rule:

To get it, say please. (*Please* didn't automatically get you what you wanted, as the kids hoped. Still, it was necessary to have any hope of getting what you wanted.)

To keep it, say, "Thank you."

When you've done something wrong, say, "I'm sorry."

Manners were particularly rewarding at restaurants. Waitresses would melt. "They are so sweet. How polite. Can I give each of them a cookie?"

I fought the urge to answer, "You really don't know if they're all that sweet. Right now, they just want to make sure they'll get their food." Instead, I said nothing. I wanted a cookie, too.

• • •

Most parents put major effort into shaping manners. "What do you say?" "How do you ask nicely?" "What's the magic word?" The drill is repetitive, exhausting even. Still, parents persevere, through thousands of prompts. Sound like an exaggeration? Give two prompts per day, and the one-year total is nearing eight hundred.

What gives manners their social weight? More than simple etiquette, it's their message: *I am treating you with courtesy because I believe you deserve it.* Manners talk respect. It's not a stretch to hear manners as a small piece of kindness.

Why then are some experts averse to forcing manners? The answer lies in the new-think that feelings reveal the genuine self. Therefore, feelings and conduct need to be in harmony. If a behavior has to be forced, the underlying feeling-motive is likely absent. The act is done from habit, or convention, or command, and as such is not fully genuine. The whole of the person is not in sync. Absent the companion internal state, the behavior is close to meaningless—unless one is angling for an extra cookie.

A similar philosophy has infected teaching children to apologize. Unless "I'm sorry" is accompanied by some honest sense of remorse, it is merely words, and shallow ones at that. Even more than manners, apologies need the proper internal state, or they too are an exercise in social rote.

Admittedly, it's easy to think this way while witnessing your son, after bombing his sister's doll house with dirt balls, mumble a half-hearted "Sorry" aimed toward the floor. It does indeed sound like an empty gesture. Even if it is, you are making a statement: *You need to offer your sister some expression of regret. Spoken responsibility is a precursor to felt responsibility.*

Not so, argue experts. Force manners or apologies against a child's will, and you'll only create a Stepford child, one who mouths the requisite formula, but who develops no internal grasp of its meaning or purpose. Put another way, "pushing" a child into *Please, Thank you, I'm sorry,* as well as other spoken social graces is a case of "no feelings, no good."

I feel like challenging this notion. To begin, human relations would be a whole lot uglier if humans didn't regularly act counter to their feelings. I may feel a powerful urge to smack the mouthy neighbor teen, but I'm wise to suppress that emotion and act against it. I may feel no desire whatsoever to acknowledge the rude waiter when he finally does bring the correct meal, but that doesn't mean thank you is not a good thing to say.

Kids don't initially embrace the motives behind much that we make them do. Think homework, chores, sharing, eating vegetables, turning off the computer, changing the toilet paper roll. The conduct is "forced" long before the reason behind it is completely understood. Connecting the internal with the external takes years, sometimes a lifetime. Simply said, you don't need to feel right to act right.

Ancient philosophers instructed: *Form the habit, the virtue will follow.* If a parent doesn't require the words, how will the habit form? Politeness isn't something kids absorb by social osmosis, even if every single grown-up around them models it. The typical child might need hundreds or thousands of repetitions before manners become second nature. Once they do, though, the virtue as well as all manner of social rewards follow.

While I was sitting in a restaurant working on this book, a mother and her daughter took a booth nearby. The waitress complimented the little girl on her cute outfit, and she stared back, as if to say, "Are you talking to me?" Whereupon, Mom intervened, "Say thank you." The little girl obliged, and the waitress offered a most pleasant "You're welcome." Smiles were exchanged all around.

Poor Mom, she didn't know she had just taught nothing. I didn't hang around long enough to see if the little girl got a cookie.

IDEA #19: DON'T USE A CHILD'S BEDROOM FOR DISCIPLINE

Why not? Is it because most kids' rooms are scale models of Disney World? Or because these kid-friendly zones are outfitted with a sixty-inch high-definition TV screen with 470 channels? Or because they contain more stuffed animals than a Toys"R"Us warehouse? In short, don't use a child's room for punishment because it offers little punishment?

None of the above. You don't do so because a bedroom is a personal place, to be associated with good feelings. It is an emotional sanctuary. Forced room time attaches negatives to what should be a positive space.

Worse, room confinement is social banishment. It is isolation from family life. It says to a child, "We are not going to talk about your behavior or your feelings right now." Supposedly, room time shares all the drawbacks of time-out, with the possible exception of boredom.

• • •

I spent lots of time in my bedroom in my youth, some of it my choice, some of it not. I don't recall fighting mixed feelings about my room. It could be both pleasant and unpleasant, depending upon why I was there. I don't seem to have any lingering ill effects from my unwilling confinements, unless one considers becoming a psychologist as evidence of trauma.

The prohibition against room time can be leveled at almost any discipline. Make Edgar Allen write essays about his bad attitude, and will he come to abhor writing? Fine Forbes a dollar for shirking his chores, and will you stunt his work ethic? Require Curt to be his little sister's servant for the next hour for treating her poorly, and are you breeding more sibling ill will?

Most discipline carries some negative element, or it wouldn't be discipline. It wouldn't teach or deter much. (And even if a child's room were to lose some appeal from forced visits, is that automatically equivalent to inflicting psychological harm?)

As with any form of time-out, the real-life pros of room time eclipse the speculated cons. In a study of strong families, "Go to your room" was a preferred discipline option, especially for older kids. None of these excellent parents expressed any reservations or worries about causing unexpected emotional distress. And none of the over three hundred children showed any.

In addition to sending young Belle to her room, I would add: Confiscate her cell phone. Otherwise, Belle can still maintain contact with the whole world. She could also barrage you with texts pleading for an early release.

Rooms afford time to think, although a child might choose instead to stew or to sleep. To put thinking to paper, assign a handwritten essay or apology. When it's completed, so is room time. Be warned, though, you could risk shaping a claustrophobic insomniac mislexic (hater of words).

Rooms afford time to cool. By separating heated parties—be they parents and kids, kids and kids, or parents and parents—all involved get time to simmer down, leaving unsaid what shouldn't be said.

Who determines duration? You. Some parents preset room time, say an automatic hour for public disobedience. Some use rooms more to calm, thus letting Peace decide when to emerge. This assumes she is truly settling and not gathering her second wind to argue.

Just because you calmly direct, "Please go to your room," doesn't mean Wally will calmly acquiesce. "Of course, Mother, did you want me to straighten it while I'm in there? Should I clean the windows, too? Do we have any shampoo for me to scrub those spots on the carpet?"

On average, the average child resists, whether a little or a lot—stalling, negotiating, defying, self-declaring "time's up." To reduce friction, here are some room rules:

1) Time doesn't begin until any verbal outpouring from the room ends.

2) Time is added if a youngster adds any nonverbal resistance before or after room time.

3) The room has to be in the same condition, or better, upon exiting as it was upon entering.

4) Outright refusal leads to immediate cessation of perks and privileges except love, some kinds of food, and, OK, the bathroom.

I like to call this last rule "blackout." The instant Chuckie challenges his time in any way—ignoring, arguing, wailing, leaving, laughing, whatever—tell him, "You have my permission to go on blackout." All right, bad phrasing. How about, "Chuckie, you are now on blackout until you serve your time—quietly." No toys, no stuffed animals, no favorite shirt, cup, or cap. No dessert, no TV, no computer, no games. No playing with friends or cousins on a visit to Grandma's. Any family outing, anywhere, Chuckie goes, but watches.

When he seeks anything on your blacklist, remind him, "Not until after you take your time-out." Which is now longer because he refused it the first time around. Don't keep re-reminding. If necessary, give him a dumb look that says, "Huh? We've been over this."

Blackout is potent parenting. With a younger child, most parents have to rely on it only a few times for short periods to get full first-time time-out cooperation.

IDEA #20: DON'T FINE A CHILD

Some experts have argued that it's a bad idea to reduce or revoke a child's allowance. After hearing this idea advanced by a media expert on relationships, and anxious to be a fiscally fair father, I tallied all the allowance money I had rescinded over the years. (When we discovered that the total was more than nine thousand dollars, the children agreed to let me make payments, with compounding interest. They knew I didn't keep that kind of cash on hand.)

What is an allowance, anyway? Is it an entitlement, or an informal contract? If an allowance is an entitlement, then the money is owed, no matter what Penny does. If it's a contract, then all parties agree to certain terms (though Penny might claim agreement under duress). If the party of the first part, hereinafter referred to as "child," breaches the contract, the party of the second part, hereinafter referred to as "parent," is not obligated to honor the original terms.

What about the experts who say that reneging on an agreement with your kid sends the message that your word can't be trusted?

Let's think about that. For years you said there was a Santa Claus. You told Ford he could drive when he reached sixteen. You once talked about sending Stanford to college in Australia. Childrearing is a fluid affair. It is constantly evolving with a child's age, responsibility, and moral maturity. And a smart parent changes with it. Doing so is not being unreliable. It is realizing a course correction is warranted. New conditions have emerged.

In most cases, it is not the parent who reneges on the allowance agreement. Rare is the parent who says, "Heloise, you've done your chores to perfection, but I now feel like giving you only half of what I said."

Much more often, it's the child who breaches it. She ignores her chores, delays them, or executes them incompetently. At that point, "Don't fine" clashes with another piece of advice: "Let the punishment fit the crime." When chores and money are linked, a reasonable response to incomplete chores is less money. It fits the crime well. It is a fair and logical result.

• • •

55

What's the best way to teach kids the value of money? Good question. There really is no one "best" way (the idea that there is definitely falls in the category of "advice worth ignoring"). Over the years I've seen parents employ three basic allowance plans.

Plan #1: "No-pay." According to this way of thinking, chores are just part of being a member of the family—though the older ones might maintain their coolness by keeping their distance from that family in public. Everyone has certain fee-free responsibilities. The house is everybody's, so its care is everybody's. Family chores might include making your bed, setting the table, doing dishes, vacuuming, fumigating your room—the basic, day-to-day operations of home life. Work for free helps prepare kids for parenthood. (Note: No-pay is the only foolproof plan if you never want to reduce a child's allowance. Since no money is ever committed, there's nothing to reduce. Rather, money is parceled according to need or given as a gift.)

Plan #2: "Money Manager." This plan has as its primary purpose learning how to budget finances. Chores may not be required. Thus, Rich might get twenty bucks a week for a token job—say, feeding the goldfish. Translated to an hourly wage, that comes to $712. Should a parent decide to impose a reduction, what would he link it to? "OK, for not feeding little Flipper, you lose fifteen dollars." (I think our expert would see that as major fiscal overkill.)

Plan #3: "Money Maker." This approach is the most popular. Housework is divided into family chores and wage chores. Certain chores are done to maintain the family, and thus are unpaid. Only certain chores are deemed "wage worthy." Family chores must be completed first. Otherwise, most kids will head straight for the money chores, leaving all else for Mom and Dad, who are supposed to work around the house for no pay.

Plan three offers the best fiscal leverage. Forbes learns that labor begets pay only if one labors first. If his clothes blanket most of the floor and sink, and you pick them up, you did his work. So the money is yours. And since you belong to Motherhood Union #172, you can charge prevailing wage. One father took an all or nothing stance: All assigned duties must be completed well to earn any pay.

Charging money works fine for other purposes, too.

Mom's toy box. Every toy you pick up is stored in your toy box, with a cost to reclaim. The amount varies by how often and how much you, the parent, had to gather. Mini-Legos would be an expensive reclamation. You'll quickly find out which possessions matter to Price and which don't. A similar system is a clothes box.

Curfew cost. Every ten minutes that Eve drifts in past curfew costs her, say, a dollar. Your rate depends, among other things, upon how much you value your sleep.

Name your price. Name-calling a sibling carries a price tag. The meaner the name, the higher the price.

Money talk. Make a list of disrespectful or mean words. Assign them a fee tied to their nastiness—twenty-five cents, fifty cents, one dollar. If Oral is going to talk cheap, it will cost her.

Paying an allowance comes with a bonus for parents. It enables us to compare our childhood to our children's. "When I was a boy, my allowance was a nickel a week. For that, I mowed the lawn, shoveled the snow—sometimes both in the same day—painted the garage, and saved for a car and my college tuition. And I was grateful for what I got."

What will our kids tell their kids? "When I was a boy, I had to empty the kitchen wastebasket on Saturdays *and* take out the trash every other Monday, all for only forty bucks a week plus benefits. And I was grateful for what I got."

The saying is true: The older we get, the greater we were.

Idea #21: Don't Punish with Writing

The story is told of a well-known author giving a speech to budding writers about how to improve at their craft. He began with advice to this effect, "What are you doing here? Go home and write."

I've been writing books for over thirty years. To this day, the self-discipline demanded in transferring thinking to writing is punishment enough without another—in my case, an editor—compelling me to do so. And so, it has always puzzled me when I come across an educator who is anti-writing as discipline, who contends that "coercing" a child to write creates a negative experience, erasing any impulse to write voluntarily, now and in the future.

More than one teacher has challenged my assertion that assigning essays can be educational. In so many words, they contest, "Don't use my subject as punishment. How would you like it if I assigned a student to read one of your books as punishment?" (I guess if they purchased it, I'd be good with that.)

I think these education "experts" are missing the big picture. After all, how does one gain skill at anything? Practice. Exceptional skill? Relentless practice—be it piano, weight-lifting, public speaking, or writing. My first book took me three years to finish; my most recent books under a year. Were they one-third the length? No. More sloppily written? I hope not. Did I have a desire to write each one? Yes. Was each a free choice? Yes. Was each a day-to-day exercise in enjoyment? No. Were all the books exercises in self-discipline, edit after reedit? Afraid so. The reward of looking at a decent finished product helped move me forward, paragraph by paragraph. A reliable writing axiom is, "If something is easy to read, it was hard to write."

• • •

In the past when I've done talks at school in-service days, I have offered the following challenge to the English and literature teachers: "Here's a proposal. Starting tomorrow, announce to your classes that you will no longer give grades. And there will be no penalty for missed assignments. All writing will be voluntary. Everyone is encouraged to write for the sheer pleasure inherent in shaping coherent sentences. At the end of one month, how many students will be turning in assignments?" Sheepish smiles circulate. The most novice teachers suspect what would happen, and it wouldn't take a whole month.

I then ask, "How is your present practice not a form of coercion? Grades and the threat of failure are external motivators. Isn't this making writing a demand backed by discipline?"

A friend completing her Ph.D. in literature told me of a professor who actually executed a proposal similar to mine. He announced to the class that as adults pursuing advanced language and writing degrees, they should no longer need anyone to "impose" writing upon them. They should be self-motivated. Therefore, there would be no formal assignments, only what each student was moved to write and when. Initially flattered, all were ready to confirm their professor's confidence in them. With each week, however, fewer pieces of writing were begun, much less finished. My friend wryly observed that even among the most motivated, writing remains a discipline and regularly needs someone or something to push it.

For most everyone, younger and older, writing is a form of exercise. And requiring someone to write—for grades, money, or discipline— doesn't "ruin" a writer. Just the opposite: It makes them practice and— who knows?—could uncover a previously undiscovered talent.

Rather than liabilities, writing as discipline comes with plenty of benefits.

One, writing can take many forms, explore many genres. It can be an essay about one's misconduct—why it is wrong, what could have been done better, what one was thinking, etc. It can be a written apology addressed to one or more offended parties. It can be a single sentence, repeated an assigned number of times. It can be looking up dictionary words, defining them, and using them in a sentence. It can be copying another's worthwhile words.

Two, writing fits the crime. It is tailor-made for misconduct in word—disrespect, nagging, interrupting, arguing, nasty language, sibling tormenting. Putting good words on paper helps redress bad words flung into the air.

Three, writing is conscience put to pen, or perhaps crayon. It is a window to a young person's mind, disclosing thoughts we may not otherwise hear. Any writing can be discussed, analyzed, pondered, and dissected. It can provide an opening to the self.

Some guidelines: Essays are not venues for argument, critique, or verbal venom. For an essay to be acceptable, it must be respectful, or it is rejected for publication. An essay is not a means to move from slander to libel.

No reiterating. My son soon realized he could multiply words by writing, "And you should not do that because God does not like it and the angels do not like it and Mom does not like it and Aunt Carla does not like it and…" We had to adjust our composition rules.

What if Edgar Allan refuses to write? Refer again to blackout—full cessation of all perks and privileges—until the essay is satisfactorily completed.

Set a limit. Imagine—if you can—that Curt won't stop arguing, and so you continue to add more words to your assignment. Cap your upper number, or else after his fifty-fourth comeback, you could fire off, "That's it, one million. Don't push me to two!"

Sometimes the humor alone is worthwhile. A mother assigned her son her standard three-hundred-word essay for his snarky arguing.

Promptly he pulled a prewritten three-hundred-word essay from his back pocket, handing it to her. He had it held in reserve for just the right time. You've got to admire his forethought.

After acting up in public, my son Andrew, about age nine at the time, wrote, "And if you act bad, people will not think your dad is a good sicologist [sic], and they won't want to hear him talk, and we won't have money to pay bills, or eat, or have a house, and I won't get to play baseball either."

From one episode of disorderly conduct, he had us homeless. Talk about conscience run amok. Andrew was in the audience when I used his example at a parent presentation. A future essay contained a "P.S.: Dad, don't use this in your talks, OK?" I told him I wouldn't. But I didn't say anything about using it in a book.

At Andrew's wedding rehearsal dinner, we shared some of his essays with his fiancée. She married him anyway.

Idea #22: Don't Make the Older Help with the Younger

A nationally known "family expert" chastened a caller who asked if she had the right to expect her older daughter to help out with a newborn sibling. (When did we start asking experts about our rights as parents?) Her answer, in so many words: *You chose to have another child. The child is yours, not your daughter's. Therefore, no, you don't have that right.*

What exactly is Mom planning to ask of older daughter? Was the poor girl to become another Cinderella, absorbing most household and maternal duties? Was she expected to spend much of her childhood caring for one or more siblings, at the expense of her own youth? If so, I could see the expert's point.

The counterpart to Cinderella would be princess. (Wait, didn't Cinderella eventually become a princess?) Meaning, the younger child is Mom's, therefore Mom's responsibility alone. Older sister is an uninvolved bystander. Perhaps every so often, under duress, she might take little sister to the bathroom at a restaurant. Helping her to get dressed? That's stretching family ties a bit too far.

• • •

Like much in life, balance applies. The caller wasn't demanding that her daughter paint her sister's bedroom or tutor her through elementary school. She wanted some appropriate family help, for her benefit as well as both children's. Reading a Dr. Seuss story to little sister would seem no heavy demand, Mom I am.

After hearing this program, an adolescent girl wrote me about how privileged she felt to be able to help out with younger siblings, calling it a blessing. She believed not only would it make her a better sister, but a better person. I copied her letter and used it to wallpaper our children's rooms. My wife copied it and used it to wallpaper my bathroom.

Studies support my young letter writer. We become better people—less self-absorbed, more other-focused—by serving. This is not something easily acquired in adulthood if it isn't fostered in childhood. Older children are not victimized serf laborers if asked to feed little Robin or to help Newton understand some arithmetic or to watch Mario show off on his bike.

My daughter Hannah is our second-oldest child and the eldest of our five daughters. She discovered early on that by helping, she could also rule. More younger siblings, more subjects. (Our older boys were only vaguely aware of littler people roaming nearby, so we had to routinely require their assistance.)

Little brothers and sisters start out idolizing older siblings. It's a natural relationship that can progress for years, assuming that the older children are forbidden to mistreat the younger. These bonds grow most durable when the older ones reach down and treat the younger with care.

Do older siblings help out on their own? Many don't. Though older, they're still kids. They need parental prompting and pushing. Nonetheless, involving them, if at times against their will, can result in rewards that become more obvious to them in time.

Parents don't rely only on persuasion or on an older child's goodwill. One family sweetened the pot, so to speak. They offered a performance bonus to their teen daughter's allowance if she potty-trained her little sister. It was to be her number-one and number-two duties.

IDEA #23: DON'T SPANK

No traditional form of discipline has gotten more grief from experts than spanking. It is far and away the most criticized, disparaged, and swatted-down of parenting practices. Parents who employ some form of corporal punishment—and to expert chagrin, that still includes a majority—are looked upon as unsophisticated, uninformed, and old-fashioned. More harshly, they are judged as mean-spirited, fear-provoking, and abusive. Spanking is childrearing public sin number one.

Our culture seems to reserve more reproach for hurting a child's bottom than it does for hurting his soul. Parents can choose to buy the most up-to-date television satellite and allow their children to watch even highly questionable channels, using their preferences as "teachable moments." Most people would be dumbfounded, of course. Some might even try to persuade that parent to rethink his plan. Still, they couldn't do anything about the sewage streaming toward those kids.

On the other hand, if you smack your preschooler's bottom for his sugar-obsessed ragings while you are out together grocery shopping, how nervously would you scour the aisle, hoping no one or no camera caught you? Upon arriving home, wouldn't you periodically scan your driveway for the appearance of some civil watchdog ordering, "Mrs. Paddlebottom, come out with all your paint sticks above your head, please."

Exaggeration? Probably. But only slightly.

Spanking has been so maligned in expert circles that even its proponents sound hesitant when endorsing it, adding qualifiers like, "Now, I don't advocate beating children" (Who does?), or, "I'm only talking about a light tap on the bottom" (Is that a spanking?), or, "Make sure you don't spank in emotion" (No emotion or no anger?). Great pains are taken to emphasize that to defend spanking doesn't tag one as an unprofessional professional.

Then too, proponents disagree among themselves. Some warn: Never spank with the hand. The hand is for affection not punishment. Others counter: Never spank with anything other than the hand. That's too close to impersonal and unfeeling. My mother used a ruler to measure my bottom more than once. When I began first grade, I was surprised to find it could be used to measure paper.

The indictments against spanking are manifold. Spanking is ineffective. Spanking teaches through force. Spanking is merely a show of power. Spanking is big people hurting little people. Spanking breeds aggressive conduct. Most ominously, spanking is a form of child abuse.

Such a litany, if true, could cause one to align with most experts. It doesn't matter, however, what I think. Nor what most experts think. What matters is: What does the research say? Unbiased, objective attempts to ask: Is any spanking whatsoever guilty of the charges leveled against it? The answer to that is *no*.

* * *

How, then, can we explain the raft of studies pronouncing spanking the cause of everything from poor self-image to aggression to future incarceration to psoriasis? OK, psoriasis isn't on the list—yet.

The simple answer lies in the word *study*. Spanking "studies" are best called "surveys." They ask people if they spank (or were spanked), how much, at what age, with what, and so forth. Even assuming that most people recall accurately—a highly questionable assumption—establishing cause and effect with surveys is very tricky. Too many other factors—researchers call them confounding variables—can intermix to explain results.

Some years back the American Academy of Pediatrics reviewed the surveys on spanking. To their surprise, they were forced to conclude that spanking, when done in good homes, doesn't lead to all the social and psychological ills theoretically linked to it. They also concluded, in so many words, "We're still against it."

That's their perspective. But that's what it is, a perspective. It is not newly uncovered hard data on the matter.

My clinical experience is consistent: Those who emotionally and erratically spank have many childrearing struggles. Parents who swing first and ask questions later also tend to have more personal problems, family instability, inconsistency, and anger. The spanking is not the sole nor even the direct cause of bad outcomes. It is one sign of troubled family life.

A TV news show placed cameras in the homes of three families, watching to capture them in the act of spanking. In two families, the discipline could best be described as weak and unsure. In one scene, after fruitless negotiation to get his young daughter to stay in bed, Father gave a "token spank"—a tentative, mostly symbolic gesture. In the third family, Mom came across as harsh and someone who, as part of her overall approach, pulled hair. Not unexpectedly, she was afforded the bulk of the interview time, with a theme of "see what spankers are like."

Let's answer some of the common objections to spanking.

Spanking is ineffective. Of course, it can be. Any discipline can be if done poorly. Time-out is ineffective if Buck serves it one of every seven times he's earned it, or if he resists by arguing, erupting, or leaving. If Dad spanks because he's "had enough," or because he's in a foul mood, or because "this time I mean it," the spanking won't teach much. It happened for reasons other than to discipline. Once again, it is not the spanking itself that is bad, it is the bad spanking.

Spanking teaches aggression. Aggressive conduct or style is a complex blend of genetics, temperament, history, and circumstances. To declare that some well-timed and well-placed swats in a child's younger years will propel him to present and future belligerence belies reason. It's similar to claiming that because a frustrated parent occasionally utters a curse word, any child within earshot will adopt cursing as his second language.

Spanking antagonists often go so far as to assert that any form of spanking, with any child, for any reason, no matter how loving the home, has ugly consequences. Only a few generations ago, corporal punishment had a presence in nearly every household. And some of that punishment would be considered excessive, if not abusive, nowadays. Certainly not to advocate a return to those days (see, I too qualify!), but can one ask: Were youth then more violent or unruly or more troubled than youth now? On virtually every measure of social pathology, the statistics say no.

A rebuttal could be that modern stressors contribute to the social troubles of today's youth. Agreed, but if one categorically claims that spanking in and of itself, independent of the quality of the home, is the culprit, then our society's history doesn't agree.

There is, it seems, more than a hint of professional arrogance involved. That is, "We moderns are finally doing it right. All the societies, cultures, clans, and people before us were ignorant in the ways of proper parenthood." Some historic practices to us do appear extreme. But did almost all people get it wrong about spanking? Was there any benefit to methods we now label psychologically incorrect, but of which the overwhelming testament of past parenthood thought otherwise?

Spanking is child abuse. The most ludicrous charge of all. Spanking and abuse are not even on the same continuum. Abuse is not meant to deter trouble or to instruct. It is lashing out with a frustrated vengeance. Abuse is cruelty; spanking is legitimate discipline. It is moderation tempered by good judgment. To equate spanking with abuse is to heap unfounded guilt of the worst kind on parents.

A real life refutation of the "spanking is always bad" notion comes from a nationwide survey of strong families. State Teachers of the Year in all fifty states nominated over one hundred families who, in their experience, were exemplary. They described their children variously as mature, responsible, of high character. Not aggressive, difficult, or challenging. Did their parents ever spank? About three-fourths did, for certain offenses and mostly when the kids were younger. Further, they viewed spanking positively, a means to ease friction rather than cause it.

The impression may be that I'm speaking up for spanking. I'm not. It is not for me to tell you how to run your family. Whether to spank is your decision. Should you decide to, here are some ideas to make spanking more effective and, thus, less frequent.

Identify the infractions that can lead to spanking. For most parents, the usual offenses include defiance, refusing other discipline, or risky behavior—conduct needing a fast stop. Our daughter Sarah was three when we adopted our twins, age four. To protest this change in our family, she began to bite, not just the twins, but anyone within reach of her fangs. Our response was spanking, then a corner time-out. Why not just time-out in the corner? Weren't we sending a mixed message: Using aggression to teach "no aggression"? Our main aim was to halt Sarah's oral aggression—like now! The corner alone would probably have worked, but after how many revisits? Twenty, thirty, more? In the meantime, twenty or more new teeth marks would have found their home on siblings.

Don't "token spank." Because having to spank sits uneasy for most parents, we lighten our hand. We go through the motions of a swat, effectively eliciting a shrug from Armstrong that says, "You wrinkled my pajamas." To have any chance to work, a spank must be felt. Otherwise, it's nonverbal nagging.

Spanking as disciplinary "spice." It should not be your go-to method of correction. Particularly with preschoolers, you can't spank enough to be consistent. They misbehave too much and too fast. The average little kid acts up slightly less often than he breathes. So, find a "workhorse" consequence for the repetitive, everyday misconduct. Reserve spanking for predetermined specifics.

Spank before overheating. Nagging, arguing, threatening, and yelling can push you quickly to your emotional limit. At that point, you're agitated, Conan's agitated, the dog's agitated, and the neighbors are agitated. Spanking becomes more a sign of frustration than a form of teaching.

In the end, spanking, contrary to all its antagonists' objections, still deserves to be judged as all discipline is judged: How well is this working, for you, for your child, in your home, and with your morals and values?

IDEA #24: DON'T OVERPROTECT

Helicopter parents. Tiger moms. Control freaks. All conjure up the image of an intrusive, dominating parent. In the extreme, the attitude is, "I'm living my life through my child," or, "My child reflects me, so I'm working to make sure my reflection looks good to others."

On the other hand, "Don't overprotect" could also mean, "Don't drive an emotional bulldozer in front of your child." Overprotecting sometimes looks like pushing aside every rock or filling every pothole that might make his road temporarily bumpy. And picking up any and all pieces from his childish miscues.

When read in either of these ways, I'm inclined to agree with "Don't overprotect." Some of the most unpleasant, hard-to-relate-to kids I've encountered are being raised by parents whose operating philosophy is, "It's not my child's fault. It's the world's fault. The world just doesn't understand my child."

"Don't overprotect" has a third meaning, however, that for the most part is ignorable: "Like it or not, it's a real world out there, and kids need to learn how to live in it, rather than being sheltered from it." Yes, it is a real world out there. And yes, kids do need to learn how to live in it. But when?

• • •

Not so long ago, the accepted wisdom was that parents should indeed overprotect their children, not only from lions and tigers and bears, but from experiencing too much of the real world too soon. Childhood was seen as a brief piece of life, and it needed to be diligently guarded by the grownups. Childhood innocence was a treasure to be secured and nurtured. It was hard to be over-vigilant.

A new mind-set now says that parents should be "realistic" about what and how soon a child should see, hear, and know things. Lag too far behind the new cultural pace, and a parent risks raising a socially awkward, out-of-place youngster. Mom and Dad are likely not to be admired for their protectiveness but instead critiqued for their overprotectiveness.

This objection is commonly leveled at homeschooling parents. It comes as a question, "What about their socialization?" The word *socialization* doesn't so much refer to the teaching of morals and character, which is and always has been a parent's role. It refers to the ongoing push-and-pull interaction with like-aged peers, even when those peers are "growing up" much faster than a parent wishes for her own child. Some socialization works against, not alongside, a parent's guidance.

Overprotective is a relative term. The most "sheltered" ten-year-old of today has likely seen and heard more social pollution than did his grandfather at age fourteen. Grandpa's parents wouldn't have been called overprotective. They would have been called responsible. A parent may look overprotective when compared to those who are underprotective.

Many twelve-year-olds today have their own cell phones, with unfettered Internet access. Most teens have televisions in their bedrooms, with dozens of cable channels. The average fifteen-year-old is dating. Going by the numbers, these are now the norms of age-driven entitlements. If one chooses to parent against the numbers, is she overprotective, or is she smart?

When you stand between your ten-year-old and the latest crude reality show, or questionable video game, or misleading peer, are you only delaying the day of moral reckoning? He will have to learn how to choose wisely eventually. Better sooner than later, the argument is, so the realities aren't such a shock to his system.

And yet, there is also a counter-argument: *Who is better able to navigate a moral minefield, a well-raised ten-year-old or a well-raised fourteen-year-old?*

Moral and emotional tests will come soon enough. Postponing their arrival doesn't stunt a child's psycho-social maturity; it gives it valuable time to stabilize and strengthen. The parent who stands strong against the cultural flow of freedoms-ever-younger will appear out of social sync. The question is not: Is my parenting in line with the new normal? Rather it is: Is my parenting abnormal, in the healthiest sense of the word?

Smarter Discipline Advice

Discipline is the hard work of childrearing. As such, it spurs more than its share of nagging questions. When do I discipline? How much? What is too strict? Too lax? How can I be calmer? More confident? More consistent?

These questions can spur self-doubt. And self-doubt can lead to vulnerability to questionable advice.

Many experts are uneasy with, or downright critical of, traditional discipline. They label it autocratic, controlling, punitive, anti-relationship, or all of the above. The image of a bigger, older person "bossing" a younger, smaller one looks so unequal, unfair even.

Discipline instruction should aim at being more cooperative and nicer. Nothing wrong with being cooperative and nice. Sometimes, though, this gentler instruction leads to less cooperation and less niceness.

IDEA #25: TIME-OUT—ONE MINUTE PER YEAR OF AGE

I confess, I get this one mixed up. Is it one minute per year of age, or one year per minute of age?

Most experts concur that some discipline is a necessary, if "negative," part of parenthood. Few would propose, "All words, all negotiation, all the time." Nonetheless, their impulse is to tone down discipline, to make it less controlling, more agreeable.

One example of this impulse is the "one minute per year of age" time-out rule, hereafter the "one-minute rule." If a parent must resort to time-out, she should limit it to at most several minutes. Above that, and she risks overdoing it.

To underscore caution, the word *brief* routinely precedes *time-out.* As in, "If Bruno trips his sister, you might give him a brief time-out." Or, "A brief time-out may teach Max not to pull the dog's ear." Parents must be reminded not to pile on the minutes, either through ignorance or frustration. In brief, keep it brief.

• • •

Once, upon coming home, I asked my wife if she had seen our six-year-old son. "Where's Andrew?" I asked her.

"Yikes!" she exclaimed. "I forgot all about Andrew." With that, she flew into the living room to find him asleep with his head cradled by the corner. Is it still one minute per year of age when asleep?

The rationale behind the one-minute rule is: The younger the child, the slower time moves for him. Three minutes feels much longer to a three-year-old than to a nine-year-old. Less time is needed to teach him the same lesson. It also limits his developmental discomfort.

Who calculated that a six-year-old can developmentally handle six minutes of time-out, but not nine or eleven? To be sure, twenty-nine minutes for a six-year-old is a stretch—she'll probably fall asleep. Along the time-space continuum, though, a parent has much room to maneuver. Little Patience is not going to be traumatized because you pushed her eight minutes beyond her supposed comfort zone.

Besides, doesn't *any* time-out more or less create discomfort within seconds? Make the experience as palatable as sitting in a recliner eating ice cream, and the discipline effect would melt.

Few children assent to being placed somewhere involuntarily. Resistance is standard—bargaining for a suspended sentence, nagging for liberty, calling for Grandma, weaseling (Mommy, can I come out and pray with you?). The typical four-year-old is just gathering his momentum at the four-minute mark. Strict adherence to the one-minute rule, in effect, says, "Go to time-out, act up, and then you're free to go."

Instead of measuring a time-out by its brevity, how about the quality of the stillness? As in, "one or more *quiet* minutes per year of age"?

My suggestion: Time doesn't start until Echo is quiet, and time starts over if she starts over.

The one-minute rule doesn't account for the severity of the infraction. Five-year-old Mason ignored your request to disassemble his block tower, blocking the toilet. Five time-out minutes. Mason disassembled his block tower over his brother's head, while brother sat on the toilet. Again, five minutes. Are both transgressions equal? Is Brother's head worth any more than five minutes? Again, a benefit of time-out is its flexibility. You can adjust it up or down depending upon the offense.

Experts often don't address the time-out question most pressing to parents: *How do I make time-out stick?* They tacitly assume Butch will cooperate because he's told.

When three of my children were in preschool, they brought home an article instructing parents how to get time-out cooperation. Their teachers, I thought, must be hearing the same discipline struggles that I hear. But their guidelines wouldn't fare too well with real kids.

If your child leaves time-out without your permission, instruct her, "You have my permission to leave."

Supposedly this returns control to the parent. Would the child hear it this way, or would she think, "Thanks for supporting me, Mom"?

Sit with your child in time-out.

Wait a time-out minute! Who misbehaved? Is Mom the one who dropped the blocks in the toilet? Did she earn the time-out? A mother sharing multiple time-outs a day would have little time to get much else done without interruption.

Play a game in time-out together.

It would seem a game is already being played—the game of, "I'll make the opening move, Mother, and then it's your turn." I don't suspect there'll be two winners.

If your child hits you, inform him calmly that hitting is "inappropriate" and that you don't like being hit.

I would imagine he already knows that. It's why he swung. (Maybe you could say, "You have my permission to hit me.")

Not one tip called for firm discipline. Raising a time-out resister (aka, a normal child) requires something stronger than, "What game do you want to play while we're sitting together on the steps?"

That's where you need blackout. (See page 54).

One mother used the one-minute rule on herself. When she acted unmotherly, she timed herself out—in her bathroom, behind a locked door, in a bubble bath. She was forty-two.

Idea #26: Create a Bedtime Ritual

What does it mean when you say, "I slept like a baby!"? Are you saying you woke up fussing every two to three hours? Did you need changing or a bottle?

Sleeping like a baby is not as restful as it sounds.

One of the first predictions offered to new parents is, "Get used to living on little sleep." Meaning, their sleep schedule will come to parallel that of little Eve's. Not to worry, though. This is a short infancy phase. After a few months, Eve should be reposing through the night, likewise Mom and Dad. For many parents, however, the phase of disrupted sleep returns in the toddler and preschool years.

At the top of preschool troubles are bedtime bad times. Not only do parents exhaust themselves maneuvering little Knap to go to bed and stay there, but after a few hours, they wake to a presence at their bedside. It becomes a nightly ritual.

• • •

My son Jon lived in foster care for about three years before we adopted him. There, Jon ruled the night, as he stalled, resisted, and roamed at bedtime and beyond. During Jon's first full weekend visit to our home, my wife proposed, "Ray, why don't you put the kids to bed tonight?"

Cornered, I thought quickly. "I'd like to, but I can't right now. I'm busy working on my parenting book. Maybe when I'm finished, sometime next year."

Her look told me I was already finished, so I called, "OK, guys, let's go. We're heading for bed."

At the time, our kids were six, five, four, four, three and one. So bedtime was about as smooth as training six Bengal tigers to walk single file backward while growling the alphabet. Eventually the kids came meandering from diverse directions, all except for Jon, who stared at me as if to say, "You're not talking to me, are you?" Clearly, bed itself was not part of his personal bedtime ritual. He punctuated his opposition with a tantrum. Temper tempests and bedtime bad times are a dynamic duo.

What would some experts advise? "Create a bedtime ritual." Set up a structured routine every night—put on jammies, brush teeth, read story, say prayers, eat chocolate cake. The steps in the routine or their number is not as central as their predictability. With repetition, Dawn will learn that bedtime is over the horizon.

Other experts add, "Set an alarm for five or ten minutes prior to bedtime." This will alert Dawn it's time to begin winding down, to transition from activity to inactivity. Thereby, when bedtime arrives, she will be agreeable, offering a goodnight kiss, an "I love you, Mommy," and smiling gratitude for your soporific transition.

Do bedtime rituals work? In my experience they do—for about 5 to 10 percent of children, mostly those who wouldn't resist bed anyway. The rest enjoy the ritual, marshal their energy, and prepare for the lightning round. The alarm clock does send a signal, one that says the real action begins in about ten minutes. Like many strategies meant to substitute for firm parenting, the bedtime ritual is designed to be more pleasant and mutually cooperative. And it would be, if it worked at nighttime like it sounds in the daytime.

Many homes do enjoy some kind of bedtime ritual. It is time shared. Only when the family completes the circuit can the ritual conclude quietly, however. Otherwise, at a certain point in the routine as the time draws closer to bed, the negotiations begin:

"I need some more water."

"Can you kiss me again?"

"Where's my other blankie?"

"Tell me another story."

"Can I say sixteen more prayers?"

"I have to pee."

When there's no happy ending, what then? Time for a backup ritual. After you say goodnight, tell Rip that if he calls, gets out of bed, argues, kicks the wall, whatever, he will leave bed and stand in the corner until you think he's ready for bed again. Repeat as needed.

If Rip won't stay in bed, why would he stay in the corner? Surprisingly, some kids do. It may have something to do with preferring the vertical to the horizontal. Still, some will view the corner like they view bed, and you are way too tired to engage. Your bedtime passed an hour ago.

Option: Move the ritual to tomorrow. Beginning at wake up, whenever Dawn seeks a privilege, respond with, "Not today, Dawn. You didn't stay in bed last night." The range of privileges to deny is up to you, somewhat depending upon how sour your mood from sleep deprivation. This approach also works well with middle-of-the-night visitors.

With either the corner ritual or the next-day ritual, most bedtime bad times smooth out within a week. Once bedtime is established, you can enjoy just about any ritual prior to it.

But what about this show-stopper? *"I'm scared."*

True or false, the plea weakens and even paralyzes the most confident parent's resolve. When bedtime becomes a blend of resistance and distress (with the exact mix nearly impossible to measure), one thing is almost certain: The more nights of resistance, the more likely some element of "scared" will evolve.

Does this change your response? In all but extreme cases, not really. Make an effort to quiet any fears—briefly reassure (*briefly* is the key word), light up the dark (two five-hundred-watt ceiling floods?), de-monster the closet and under the bed, provide Superman or Wonder Woman protective stuffed animals or a guardian angel picture. Then respond as above to the remaining resistance.

What if the fear is more real than not? Most kids still quickly pass through it once it is no longer kept alive by nightly agitation. Falling asleep faster leaves less time to think oneself into distress. It's hard to be nervous when you're asleep.

Back to Jon. How did I get him to bed? I used a highly sophisticated behavioral strategy. Carrying Jon to bed, I firmly held him there, promising to let go when he calmed. No time for rituals, corners, or next-day consequences. I had to make Jon stay in bed the first night, as he could be a safety risk for himself and us if he were to explore the house unsupervised.

Andrew, my six-year-old son, was watching the whole scene from his perch on a top bunk. "Andrew, would you please talk to your brother?"

"Jon, you better stay in bed because Daddy means it. I remember one time I didn't stay in bed, and if you don't either, you're not going to like it. You think Daddy will leave? He won't. He'll stay out in the hall, and if you get up…"

"OK, Andrew, that's plenty."

At age six, Andrew already could lecture like a dad. He'd better learn to squelch the impulse at his kids' bedtime, though.

IDEA #27: REWARD THE POSITIVE, IGNORE THE NEGATIVE

It's Behavior Theory 101: Reward a behavior, and you get more of it. Ignore a behavior, and you get less of it. You starve it of whatever social oxygen is feeding it.

Not too many people need academia to teach them the power of positives. That has been known since Adam and Eve. The soul of strong family life is wrapped throughout with positives—love, affection, praise, commitment. The more a child receives the positives, the less he gives the negatives. So why is this advice worth ignoring?

It's the second part of the equation that's problematic. "Ignore the negative" is based on the assumption that much negative behavior, or misbehavior, is done to seek attention. It aims for a response—positive or negative. The premise is: Children want attention. And negative attention is better than no attention. If this premise is faulty, and misconduct has multiple motives other than to seek attention (such as, "I want to do what I want to do"), then ignoring it won't halt it, not in the short term anyway. Instead, ignoring it will likely prolong it in the long term.

Whether facing a four-year-old's emotional flare-up or a fourteen-year-old's verbal one, some would counsel: *Ignore it, depart from the scene, attend to the dog, plug your ears while singing "Sounds of Silence." Do whatever you can to stay oblivious.* Oscar will soon see that his performance is getting no audience reaction, and he'll cancel it.

Perhaps, but when? In five minutes? Twenty-five? Tomorrow? The curtain may indeed come down—not because you exited stage left, but because Oscar has run out of lines for this episode.

• • •

Does ignoring ugly drama discipline it? If you stoically endure Talulah's nasty lines, is she being held accountable for them? Has she been taught anything other than that nothing will happen? Actually, something does happen—you get mistreated.

Much misbehavior needs to be corrected rather than ignored.

"Barrymore, please calm down, or you will calm yourself on your bed for the next hour."

"This is disrespectful badgering, Gabby. For it, you will write twenty reasons why you're grateful to live here."

"That was a big fit, Storm. The next five things you ask for will get a no."

In other words, when seeking to terminate negative behavior, action generally works better than inaction.

What if you remain stoic, and the misbehavior gains momentum? As soon as Emmy realizes she's getting ignored—within about ten seconds or so—she becomes harder to ignore. Rather than abating, ignored behavior often surges in volume and emotion.

What if Chase pursues you? You walk away, and he walks away with you. He is not finished yet. He has more to share. Where can you hide? When will your stamina crack? Most of us have a limit to our obliviousness—a limit generally reached sooner than a child tires. Hitting our limit, we react, usually badly, rendering our previous oblivion for naught. Put another way, we may not be able to ignore Constance as long as she can persevere. Acting before frustration overwhelms us keeps our own misbehavior to a minimum.

Parents proclaim, often proudly, "She pushed hard on me, but I didn't give in." Or, "He nagged at me for over an hour, but I kept tuning him out." Granted, perhaps Howland didn't win what he wanted from his prolonged pressure, but what did you lose? Your peace? Your family's peace? How much did you have to withstand before his energy subsided? Ignoring nastiness from an adult may be wise. Ignoring it from a child—one you are responsible for socializing—is not.

Reward the positive; ignore the negative, *if* the negative doesn't need discipline.

IDEA #28: PUNISHMENT DOESN'T TEACH

This was a line I was taught in graduate school. I memorized it in no time, too—they threatened me with a poor grade if I didn't learn and agree with the theory.

To teach well, the theory continued, one must rely on positives—praise, encouragement, rewards, token systems. "Trophies for everyone" and the self-esteem movement are byproducts of this thinking.

Punishment supposedly teaches only one thing. It teaches the punished to avoid the punisher. No other lesson is internalized.

• • •

One needn't be a college prof to know that good parenthood is filled with more positives than punishments. Most guidance is grounded in love and affirmation. Still, even if you affirm the good every minute, you will still have to confront the bad. Pardon the value-laden language.

How does this theory define *punishment?* It is an unpleasant or "aversive" action imposed upon a behavior. Spankings and time-outs would both fall under this broad umbrella, according to some experts. What else might be considered punishment? Grounding? Loss of privileges? Fines? Extra chores? Push-ups? No red M&Ms?

No doubt, these are aversive to most kids, despite comebacks of "I don't care." None would a child choose to do in her free time. "Mom, I'm feeling a little guilty about not drying the dishes for you tonight. So here's a quarter before I head for bed. And tomorrow, do you mind if I weed the flowerbed to make up for my slacking off?"

A word sometimes used for punishment is *consequences.* Do consequences teach little or nothing? Do they merely give a parent the sense that she is shaping morals and character by using them? Granted, some kids do lower their profile when sensing discipline is near. Is this "avoiding the punisher"? Or is it merely self-interest?

It's an immutable truth: Life teaches by both reward and punishment. Parents imitate the teaching of life, albeit with more loving, kinder hands. If a parent doesn't discipline now, for whatever reason—guilt, apathy, fear of psychological incorrectness—the world someday will. And the world doesn't worry about how it punishes. It teaches rough. Few parents teach as hard as life, even when they punish strictly.

If punishment or consequences are futile, why are well-disciplined children more mature and pleasant to be around? Are these effects illusory? The actual effect of a childhood without punishment will be a child anxious to flee his parents as soon as he is old enough. What do both common sense and reality teach?

They teach: The more willing a parent is to discipline, and that some-times means punish, the less she has to discipline. The more calmly confident her authority, the less she has to assert it. Reluctance to punish when called for does teach. It teaches a youngster to be unruly and unpleasant. In turn, he'll teach others to avoid him. Then he will be socially punished.

IDEA #29: LET HIS DISTRESS BE HIS DISCIPLINE

A mother sought my help with her son, Sam, who at age seven was still throwing the picturesque tantrums of a three-year-old. Sam had previously been in counseling for his "anger-management issues" (the reigning psychological catchphrase for poor self-control), but Mom lamented that Sam's self-control was getting poorer.

No surprise, as most oppositional kids don't benefit all that much from individual therapy. They respond more quickly to better parenting, notably better discipline. The main change agent is the parent. She is far more motivated and able than the little one, and when she improves, typically so does her child.

Mom described a particularly fiery episode while in the car. I asked what she did about it. She said, "Nothing." Sam's therapist had told her that his agitation was his correction. His distress was discipline enough. She didn't need to add anything else.

"Do you agree with this?" I asked. Mom was unsure. Her instincts told her to discipline, but the professional told her not to.

• • •

No question, temper eruptions at any age, seven or seventy, can incite all kinds of distress. At age thirteen, in a surge of anger, I punched a wall, promptly breaking my hand. My unbridled emotion wasn't my punishment; my fractured knuckle was. My parents didn't discipline me. They neither wanted to nor had to. Besides, when Mom saw the cast, she felt really sorry for me.

Intense emotions regularly precede foolish behavior, mostly the unthinking, impulsive kind. Intense emotions also follow foolish behavior. For the same behavior, however, it is unlikely that the same emotion is both cause and effect. My fist-to-wall collision was driven by frustration. One instant post-impact, the frustration was gone, replaced by pain and a sense of stupidity as well as embarrassment.

Sam's therapist was counting on his upset to "teach" him that his tantrums weren't worth it. Maybe a grown-up might learn that. But would a seven-year-old? What if Sam thought he was entitled to his anger? As he felt it, his reaction was a natural response to being unfairly denied or thwarted. After an outburst, even we older folks don't always experience pure regret. Usually in the mix is some sort of justification.

Then again, if distress does double as discipline, one could expect that self-defeating conduct would fade over time. How much negative emotion can a person endure before starting to change his ways? All manner of self-injury—anger, alcoholism, inveterate gambling, pornography—could be overcome through the relentless assault of bitter after-emotions. Some people do shed entrenched bad habits after accumulating misery. Others need other hands to pull them from their dead-end paths.

Many experts see temper outbursts as emotional expressions: outward signs of inner turmoil. As one put it, "His emotions are bigger than he is." As such, a parent's best response is no response. She should endure the heat until it cools. Let Blaize's agitation be a learning experience for her.

Temper is routinely more than frenzied emotions. Partnering with them are hurtful words, roaring volume, and assaults—toward property or people. The whole scene is not merely one of emotional drama. Allowing a tantrum to run its course with no follow-up discipline can send a silent message: Act wild and your only discipline will be self-inflicted. Just send a signal when you're done.

Let-it-all-loose eruptions are primarily the hallmark of two- and three-year-olds, or they should be. Unfortunately, tantrums from five-, ten-, and twenty-year-olds are a main reason parents seek my counsel. Though their youngster may be generally unruly or defiant, it is his outbursts that are rocking the home scene. Parents see them as extreme and question what is "wrong" with their child. Most of the time, nothing is wrong. Mom or Dad or both have underestimated—sometimes for years—the resolute firmness needed to slowly extinguish these flares.

As we shared earlier, we adopted our son Jon when he was four. His earliest years were marked by erratic and permissive discipline, which fueled a raging style when others or life didn't act as he wished. During Jon's first weeks with us, my wife desperately looked for some common trigger to his tantrums. Being a professional observer, one day I announced, "I think I've discovered Jon's trigger—he's breathing." So frequent were Jon's rants that we implemented a multi-consequence approach.

Our first consequence was a corner time-out. Then we added others. For example, the next privilege Jon wanted was met with, "I would have let you, Jonny, but not after carrying on like you did." The answer was the same for the next two, three, or several privileges, depending upon the intensity of the tantrum. Pretty potent stuff, right? And it did work fast. In only a year or so, the tantrums subsided to near zero.

A temper display might also earn an automatic "blackout." The length of the blackout depends upon how ugly and how long the tantrum was and the child's age. The littlest children regularly emotionally unravel, as their self-restraint is fragile. Moving toward five or six, though, most kids are capable of enough self-control to not totally lose it when frustrated. For them, a tantrum becomes more willful than spontaneous. It is not unreasonable to give a week of blackout for a nasty or violent outburst from a teen.

To summarize: One, an agitated state can be the *cause* of an outburst, not necessarily its effect. Two, what looks to an observer to be a terribly unpleasant emotional upset may not feel quite the same way to the "performer." Three, ugly actions don't always lead to regret. Sometimes they result in self-satisfied justification. Four, most children can't learn on their own to control runaway emotions, no matter how distressing. They need parent-imposed control. Over time they will develop self-control.

IDEA #30: ALWAYS GIVE A WARNING FIRST

A popular classroom discipline program touts itself as "back to basics" and "no nonsense." It relies much upon warnings and begins with a listing of classroom rules in positive language. No "nos" or "don'ts."

If a student breaks a rule, she writes her name on the board. That serves as her warning. A second infraction earns a checkmark beside her name, along with a mild consequence, say, five minutes of reduced recess. At the end of the day, all names and checkmarks are erased.

Assume a class has twenty students. If every child realizes he's granted one warning per day, over a 180-day school year, this strict program would allow 3,600 instances of misconduct with no consequences other than a name written in chalk. It's a good thing most kids don't do the math.

Well, most of them don't.

My son's second-grade class used a similar system. Every child began the day with a series of colored cards—green, yellow, and red.

All started in green. Break a rule, and you flipped your card to yellow, signaling caution or warning. Again, twenty kids and 180 school days equal 3,600 assorted rule violations with only a yellow card resulting.

The first day of school, Andrew came home giddy. "Dad, I can get in trouble once every day and nothing happens."

I concluded the system could use some fatherly tinkering.

I gave Andrew a week to adapt to the program, after which a yellow would lead to a home response. How would I know about any color change? His teacher agreed to send home a brief note. If she forgot, another female stood ready to inform me—Andrew's first-grade sister. I never could quite figure out how she always knew what Andrew did mere minutes after he did it, from four classrooms away. But she always knew.

• • •

Repeat warnings are a variant of nagging. And nagging reiterates a discipline truth: The more you talk, the less you're heard. Warnings have a way of piling upon themselves, leading to more warnings and less action. After a week of daily reminders, does Felina really not yet know she shouldn't call her brother "dog-breath"? After a month of card-flipping, does Art truly not yet understand he shouldn't abandon his colored pencils all over the family room floor?

Of course they do.

Warnings invite misbehavior. Andrew, upon realizing he had a daily freebie, was open to using it. After all, he reasoned, the only discipline would be a color shift. He could live with that—a small price for added liberty. I had to warn him that's not how Dad colored things.

When parents substitute warnings for actual discipline, their authority quickly erodes. One of the most common struggles parents face is disrespect—in words, tone, looks. I will ask, "What do you do when your son does that?"

"Well, I tell him, 'Do not use that tone of voice with me, young man.'"

"Then what do you do?"

"He hears me loud and clear that I will not tolerate disrespect."

"No. What do you *do*?"

About my third or fourth, "What do you do?" the parent will hear my point: He has been mostly just reissuing warnings. The warning has become the discipline.

Let's say Max is tormenting the dog. "Stop it, Max. He is not bothering you." Warning number one. Max then stops for about twenty-two seconds before reengaging.

"Max, I'm not telling you again. Get away from him before you get nipped." Warning number two—a dual warning, a warning that Dad is not about to rewarn. Sensing Dad's agitation, Max ceases. Six minutes later, Spot is again getting dogged.

"Max, what did I tell you?"

Hear the cycle? Upon being warned, Max does stop, temporarily. Dad believes that Max is listening, but the listening is short-lived. Dad's voice no sooner fades than Max recommences his harassing. Doing little to deter Max, the warnings have become a substitute for action. Dad could have said, "Max, bother the dog again, and you'll be in your room where you can't bother him." Still a warning, but now a prelude to discipline.

That's the difference between a *warning* and a *forewarning:* the prospect of a specific and immediate consequence.

Some years ago my wife and I had an appointment with an attorney. As we trooped into the immaculately furnished office with our children, a look of terror flashed across the receptionist's face. All she saw (and probably smelled) were six kids under age six who looked like within minutes they could depreciate the office by several hundred dollars.

Scanning the kids, I directed, "All right, guys, find seats." Like football players breaking a huddle, they scattered to couches and chairs. "I'm impressed," said the receptionist.

"Don't be," I said. "You didn't hear the warning I gave the kids in the hall." Or for that matter, the countless warnings I'd given over the years before entering a wide array of places—restaurants, sporting events, Grandma's house, the courtroom (kidding!).

Did my forewarnings work? Did they head off potential trouble spots? About 50 percent of the time—a pretty good success rate whenever kids are involved.

A forewarning is not a threat. It is a straightforward statement of expectations. If you do X, I will do Y, at first opportunity. A forewarning actually lowers the probability of having to discipline.

Neither, as some experts warn, does a forewarning give a child the idea to misbehave. Meaning, if you tell Ripley what you'll do if he does X, you've just given him the impulse to do X. As if he's never thought about it or acted on it before. Kids don't need our input to concoct ways to act up. As they would be quick to inform, "I'm perfectly capable of figuring out where and how to cause trouble, thank you very much."

At the risk of repeating myself, a last warning: Warnings have a tendency to multiply. Reserve your warnings for new stuff or situations where new stuff may happen. For the frequent, high-profile misconduct, no warning is necessary. Action is.

IDEA #31: PICK YOUR BATTLES

Our family vehicle was a fifteen-passenger van. Every time we ventured out on the open road, I got this nagging feeling of discipline impotence. The kids in the very last seats might as well have been in the next area code for all that my voice could reach back there.

As the length of the trip increased, so did the chances the kids would sing. Happy family sounds, right? Not every time. Having an overinflated sense of their musical skills, each child belted out different songs, with made-up words, off-key, all striving for the lead soprano. The cacophony rivaled that of the macaw cage at the zoo.

However ear assaulting it was, the kids weren't misbehaving. My wife and I let them drone on for a while (about fifty-four seconds on average). We tried not to react, unless you call turning up the radio a reaction.

But we had our limits, of course. When she and I wanted to hear ourselves talk, or were entering a drive-through, or were passing a state trooper who could pull us over for excessive noise, the announcement rang out from the front seat: "OK, kids. Time to tone it down."

With that, the conditions inside the van changed. No more crazy singing. It was time to obey Mom and Dad. In short, the battle front shifted.

• • •

"Some things I just let go." I hear parents say this all the time. It can be good not to get too caught up in the stuff of childishness, for your own sanity and to conserve energy. So much of what kids do is not wrong, or hurtful, or defiant, or dangerous, or irresponsible. It may bother us. We may prefer it didn't happen. But does it demand discipline? Not always. Decide what needs your attention and what doesn't. Judge what calls for discipline and what doesn't, based on your values and convictions.

When Neilson watches television, he squirms, twirls his hair, and looks backward through his legs while resting on his head. His viewing habits are silly, but are they wrong? He's being a boy, in full mode. The action isn't battle-worthy unless his backside blocks the TV or his various vocal renditions interrupt family viewing. (If you're like most parents, you've likely wished for a remote with a mute button that works on children.)

Be careful, though. When the experts say to "pick your battles," they are actually saying: *Stand firm on major moral matters, but be flexible on the minor ones, especially if your youngster overall is "a pretty good kid."*

Suppose Harmony regularly opines about your rules, in edgy words, nasty tone, and huffy body language. Very likely, ignoring her behavior won't improve things between you. But which expressions are discipline-worthy? Ugly language, insults, curse words? What would be minor salvos and thus ignorable? The eye rolls, disgusted sighs, the *whatevers?* Major or minor, isn't all of it disrespect? Or do you draw a line between mild mistreatment and harsh mistreatment? Where do you draw the line between discipline and retreat (i.e., ignore or endure)?

This same principle applies to other areas as well. For example, if you're the parent of a boy, one with a bedroom, I suspect you've heard some battle-weary advice like:

"Just close the door."

"You should see my son's room."

"If that's your biggest problem, count your blessings."

Should you surrender on the room battle? Up to you. But should you choose to drain the swamp, that too is up to you. It may appear to be a small skirmish in the overall scheme of things, but you believe it actually looms larger than that. You also don't want to provide an environment for unclassified life forms.

My advice? Where your child's morals and responsibility are concerned, if someone advises you to pick your battles, ignore him. Don't pick his advice.

IDEA #32: LET SIBLINGS WORK OUT THEIR CONFLICTS

Let's say I'm a nine-year-old boy. My sister is six. I'm bigger, stronger, feistier, and slicker (maybe). Is it in my interest to accommodate? Or would I be inclined to solve conflicts in my favor? Is self-love stronger than sibling love?

Can you imagine my nine-year-old self saying to my sister, "OK, Harmony, let's try to work this out. Since I'm the big brother, I will sacrifice. You play with the Legos first, all by yourself, for the next fifteen minutes. No, wait, make it twenty. I remember what it was like to be six. It's easy to be ignored. Then I'll take my turn for twenty minutes. After that, we'll play together. See, isn't that better? And Mom can enjoy her nap."

If by some quirk of nature, you have a child like this, I'd say let him solve all conflicts. In fact, I'd say let him raise himself—and his sister, too.

• • •

What sibling, little or big, is going to think like this? It's not natural. Not for adults, and not for youth. (If it were natural, there wouldn't be so many high-priced motivational speakers telling everybody how to construct win-win scenarios.)

The experts call the everyday sibling bickering and clashes "sibling rivalry." *Rivalry* connotes contention, an ongoing competition for attention, privilege, perks. It's a supposed given of the relationship. How likely, then, for kids to peacefully work things out when percolating rivalry lurks beneath?

A more fitting description would be sibling quibbling or sibling squabbling. Consider the facts. Two or more partially socialized, partially moralized beings living in close proximity for years are asked to get along. With mutual immaturity, each jostles for the upper hand— sometimes cooperatively, sometimes not.

As the oldest of four children, I'd have been thrilled had my mom and dad allowed us to solve our own clashes. In the sibling rankings, I saw myself on top; therefore, I should set the agenda. Given that, I never could quite figure out how my sisters so regularly outmaneuvered me. Only years later did I realize that older doesn't necessarily mean smarter.

In smooth-running families, mutual respect is the oil. Each person is expected to treat every other person well. It won't always happen, but it's an ideal. Would it be wise to put fraternal correction in juvenile hands? Would it be wise to let one child set the other's curfew? Bedtime? Allowance? No parent would permit this. It's the same with respect. In the main, children are not well-suited to guide other children to respectful engagement.

Sibling quibbling is a high-frequency misbehavior. It can erupt hourly (minutely?). Understandably, we are tempted, whenever and however, to stand back, hoping the pugilists call a truce, however uneasy. Battle fatigue can tempt us to take on an observer role.

Our ten children were all under our roof for several years. I never ran the numbers, but all the possible combinations of feuding parties had to run into the billions. My wife and I were sometimes slow to intervene. Not because we harbored any illusions about their making peace on their own. Mostly it was because of our own ignorance: We didn't know who started it, who prolonged it, who was lying, and whose crying was faked.

We toyed with installing a whole-house, eye-in-the-sky camera so we could review the tapes for real-time input, until we realized we already had one—an eight-year-old daughter. "Father, I have some information you might be interested in. It concerns a boy whose name begins with *J*, and how he tripped a girl whose name begins with *E*. Aren't you glad I'm here to help?"

Experts contend that letting siblings forge a consensus helps them hone conflict-resolution skills. The conflict itself provides a venue for maturing, compelling each to be negotiable. The idea has appeal—in books. Flesh-and-blood kids don't always read experts' books. For one, the dominant child—again, not synonymous with oldest—is not about to willingly surrender his "rights" while he masters negotiating skills. That may be what grown-ups want for him, but it's not what he wants.

For another, most conflicts are not resolved equally. There is a victor and a vanquished. Even should kids ultimately call a truce, what could happen along the way? How much volume and ill-temper? How many names called? Hurt feelings or hurt bodies? The sibling bond is durable and can absorb a lot of pounding. But that doesn't mean the pounding is good for it.

Some parents referee when the fracas moves toward the physical. Some, when it reaches a certain pitch. Some, when the chaos forces them to come out of the bathroom. And some, when there is crying— by a child or a parent.

Siblings are better able to solve it themselves if the parent sets the terms of engagement. Resolution can be pursued within certain parameters—no hitting or pushing, no put-downs, no jumping off the ropes. Though the kids could see such limits as stifling their creativity. Whenever and however you decide to involve yourself, here are some tips for honing your own conflict resolution skills.

1) When faced with a he said-she said, he did-she did, don't try to ferret out who did what to whom, when, where, and how much. Loud stereophonic discord can damage your eardrums.

Harmony: Mom, he keeps looking at me every time I work my puzzle.

Justice: I never looked at you. Why would I? Your face looks like the dog's, and it's got more slobber, too.

Harmony: See, that's how he talks all the time when you're not around. All I did was go to the bathroom, and he starts moving my puzzle pieces.

Justice: That's not your puzzle. Grandma bought it for both of us.

Besides you were in the bathroom forever. Who do you think you are—Dad?

Charity (entering the room): Hey, what are you guys doing with my puzzle?

When you can't figure it out, don't want to, or don't have the time (you do have a doctor's appointment next week), all parties meet the same discipline—corner, puzzle removed, writing twenty-five nice things about each other.

"There's not twenty-five nice things about him!"

"Make them up, then."

2) Sometimes you may have to make an educated guess as to who created more conflict than resolution. Indeed, much of parenting is educated guesses. Consequences are distributed according to your estimate of responsibility.

3) Don't expect to hear agreement with your solution. The f-word ("fair") will be flung at you from all parties. At least you've got them cooperating on that. Your goal is not to be perceived as fair, but to effect a settlement, or at least a cease-fire.

Teaching kindness and respect is not a brother's or sister's role. While they may learn some from each other, the main socializer of a child is a parent, not another child. You are far better at being a parent than they are, despite what they think.

Idea #33: Overlook a Messy Bedroom

Eight teenagers have moved through my home on their way to adulthood, with two still in residence. No official inspections have ever taken place, but I would guess certain bedrooms in my house were flirting with multiple city health code violations. At a minimum, citations from the EPA.

Here are other parents' accounts.

"I won't go in there without hazmat gear."

"Two of her sisters accidently stumbled into her room about a week ago, and we're still searching for them."

"We call his room Star Trek: to enter is to 'boldly go where no mom has gone before.'"

What is it about kids and bedrooms that elicits such exaggeration or, as some might argue, such truth? Too much stuff? Shaky work ethic? Minimal sense of ownership? No time to straighten?—Right.

Whatever the explanatory mix, the ruined-room phenomenon is so pervasive and frustrating that parents are tempted to surrender and admit defeat. Experts concur: "Don't engage in a contest of wills. Pick your battles. Focus on the major issues."

Kids echo the experts. "Why are you always on me about my room? I get good grades. I'm not on drugs. And I don't get in trouble." Translation: "I'm a great kid, and you should be grateful. Why do I have to clean my room, too?"

• • •

In a limited sense, it *is* Dusty's room, if that means "his individual place." In most other senses, it is *your* room. Is he renting it or making a house payment? Does he share the cost of electricity, heating, cooling, furnishings? Did he buy the new carpet or paint to maintain it? No? He may claim ownership, but house ownership trumps room ownership.

How you wish to view Dusty's room is your business. I know, through binoculars. One option might be simply to close the door. (Install a steel one. Animals can gnaw through wood.) As the parent, however, you have every right to expect, yes demand, that the room meets your idea of orderliness.

Suppose Comfort is indeed an honor student, class president, soccer captain, and in her spare time knits shawls for ladies in the nursing home. Isn't that enough? Can't you let her room slide? You could. Does the fact that she is in most things a sweetheart allow her to pick and choose where she cooperates? "I'm a good child, so don't ask me to be neat, too."

I wonder if I could try this kind of logic on my wife: "You say I'm a good husband and father, so why do I have to mow the lawn, too?" In other words, "You should be pleased with how wonderful I already am."

Of course, you could choose to lower your expectations just to be like other parents. "That's just teens; they're all like that." Or, "Compared to my son's room, your daughter's is the White House Greeting Room." Or, "Don't get upset over nothing. I quit getting bothered by his room two years ago."

On the other hand, don't let the opinions of other parents pressure you to relent in an area that you feel is important to your child's future happiness or success. Is your child constantly losing homework, sports gear, and family pets? Does the smell of dirty laundry waft out into the family area? You have every right to expect your children to show consideration for others.

What if you've pushed, prodded, pleaded, and threatened to truck in a backhoe and haul out and burn the refuse in the backyard, all to minimal effect? The room is still barely habitable.

As always, enforcing a standard calls for action.

1) Clean the room yourself, but charge for your time. What is maid service worth per hour? Do you have a recycling fee?

2) Using an extra-large trash bag, sort through the room's wreckage. Inform Clay of your plan, warning him that you can't really know what's valuable and what isn't. Who knows what would end up in your bag?

3) When Freeman asks for a privilege, link it to his room's condition. "Is your room clean?"

4) Set up inspection times. Say, Wednesday at 6:00 PM and Saturday at 10:00 AM. Sandy can't leave his room until it is straightened to your satisfaction.

5) Fine Penny a set amount for every day that her room is in disarray. This will help offset any depreciation to your house.

There's a benefit to a trashed room. If you run out of storage space in the garage, you can always park the lawn tractor at the end of Dusty's bed. He'll never know it's there.

IDEA #34: ALWAYS GIVE YOUR REASONS FOR RULES AND DISCIPLINE

Despite appearances, children aren't real creative in their misbehavior. Several basics account for much of the trouble: disrespect, sibling quibbling, chore-shirking, homework hassles, temper tempests, bedtime bad times, meal ordeals. Some kids do have their own signature misconduct, but even that can become recurrent with time.

Because parents want to believe that children are at the core rational creatures, we keep explaining the rules and the reasons for those rules. We want to believe that, given enough time and effort, we can give kids sufficient rationale, and they will hear, agree, and cooperate.

That's the theory. The reality is something very different.

• • •

During family counseling, I will ask a youngster, "Why do you think your mom [or dad] disciplines you for [fill in the blank]?" From kids as young as preschoolers, I usually hear more than the default "I don't know." Age-insightful answers include:

"They want to teach me to do the right thing." Or, "They love me and are trying to raise me right."

Teens may offer a different slant, "They say they want the best for me." (Note the "they say." At least they can recite our words.)

Whereupon, I take out smelling salts to revive the stunned parents, who mumble, "Why does he argue with me so much then?" I reply, "It's not that he can't repeat what you've repeated all these years. It's that he doesn't like it."

Most children don't need all that much time to hear, even comprehend, parents' motives. However, they may need most of a childhood to agree and cooperate. At their age, we simply can't expect them to see things as an adult does.

If a juvenile saw life through adult eyes, he wouldn't need us for much other than love, food, and shelter. Every few months we could impart some bit of wisdom, "Remember, Newton, always do your math homework. At your age, you don't know what career you'll someday pursue, so keep all your options open, OK?"

"I agree, Father. In fact, I'm going to frame those very words on my bedroom wall."

Kids are experts at pushing parents into never-ending rationales. "Why? Just give me one good reason," they command.

Good reason? By whose definition? What is a perfectly good reason to us isn't to them. If Wiley truly wanted a good reason, wouldn't we be rewarded with something like, "OK, Mom, now that you put it that way, I get it. Your logic is compelling." At least every year or so?

By asking for reasons and summarily rejecting them, kids are revealing their intent. They are not so interested in our *why* as in their *why not.*

How much do you repeat yourself? If the answer is, "Till they get it," you can probably cease today. They get it, if that means being able to quote you. If it means acting upon their understanding, then they probably don't fully get it. They're still maturing.

Can you stop all explaining? Not completely. New pieces of misconduct arrive with each age. For everyday stuff, though, don't exhaust yourself. "Now, Beauregard, why is it wrong to call your sister a doofus?"

I've got to believe he's known why since the first time you asked. He just likes the name.

Over-explaining obeys the law of diminishing returns. The more you explain to Justice, the further apart both of you get. He'll answer with more arguing, justifications, excuses, and blame-throwing. Like adept fencers, kids can ward off a parry of words from every angle, no matter how skilled the words.

A guideline when disciplining repeat misbehavior: *The less said, the better.* You'll receive less kid logic.

"Because I said so, that's why!" Some years ago I came across a headline that screamed "The Ten Worst Things You Can Say to Your Kids!" Nervous about reading further, I could only imagine what might sit on that list. I needn't have worried. "Because I said so" made the top ten, as well as some other similarly benign phrases. If these are really the worst things that could be said, most parents, me included, would earn top-ten-worst communicator status.

"Because I said so" (BISS) is seldom a parent's first reason. After traipsing through thirteen other reasons, none of which are accepted, a frazzled parent erupts with "Because I said so, that's why!" At which the child—usually an adolescent—retorts, "Oh, that's a good reason. I'll never say that to my kids." Of course he will, almost guaranteed, especially if someday he has a child just like him. When no explanation suffices, the temptation is to rely upon one of "the ten worst."

Then too, BISS is an honest answer. Many decisions for your child's well-being boil down to your judgment. Bedtime at eight thirty rather than ten? No television on school nights? No cell phone at age thirteen? No burping the alphabet at the dinner table? All are grounded in a parent's discretion. Yes, you have other reasons. But underneath it all, you decide what's best for your home and family. And sometimes you say so.

Why should you listen to anything I've said? I think I gave you some good reasons. If none are persuasive, how about, "because I said so"?

IDEA #35: MAKE THE PUNISHMENT FIT THE CRIME

Punishment is not a favorable word in today's childrearing lexicon. It connotes being negative and unfeeling. Neither should childish misconduct be called a *crime*. That, too, is quite linguistically harsh. Nonetheless, the sound bite is used to advise.

What exactly does it mean? As far as is possible, one should relate any discipline to the infraction that preceded it. The closer the connection, the better the lesson adheres. The savvy parent should search for consequences most appropriate to the trouble.

Sometimes this includes relying on "natural consequences," that is, results that flow readily from a behavior. Disobey Grandma when she is babysitting, and she may not babysit next time—and she will keep her cookies, pies, and ice cream at home. Leave Rollerblades in the driveway, and the overnight rain could ruin their wheels. Belittle Mom, and she might just abandon the conversation, ending Charity's negotiating for platform shoes.

A parent doesn't have to do the actual disciplining. The laws of nature—physical or social—will do it. As Prudence comes to realize that her A leads to life's B, she will alter her A.

Up to a point, perhaps. Even so, in the above examples, both Grandma and Mom are mistreated. Should that evoke anything more than a natural consequence? Is the tacit message: *"Act rudely, I'll just leave the scene"*?

A parent will tell me that when his teen's words or tone go sour, he walks away, or tries to. Often the child trails him; she isn't finished yet. He's seeking my counsel for two reasons: One, the bouts of disrespect keep increasing, and two, so does his irritation. Dad's retreat—the natural consequence—is doing little to hold his teen accountable for her conduct.

Consider the rained-on Rollerblades. Who paid for them? In 98.2 percent of cases (my unofficial estimate), a parent did. It's a rare nine-year-old who buys his own Rollerblades, or bike, scooter, lawn games, or speedboat. Consequently, Price's neglectful loss of possessions is also his parent's loss. Here the natural consequence impacts the parent, too.

One could counter, "Don't replace the Rollerblades." Again, my unofficial estimate is that 98.2 percent of parents may stay that course for a month, maybe more, but eventually they will replace them. And if they don't, Grandma will.

• • •

Parents long-time flummoxed with a child's long-time ducking and dodging of schoolwork will sometimes turn to life for help. "OK, Cornell, if you don't want to do your work, your grades will show it. And eventually you will fail and repeat the year. Your choice." Sadly, the child does make his own choice, often a bad one. He doesn't weigh the natural consequences until they happen.

The experts also advise: Make the consequence logical. Find one most tailored to the infraction. For example, abuse a privilege, and you lose it. Track mud on the carpet, and you vacuum. Kick your brother in the shin, and you'll carry him on your back to the bus stop. OK, you can use a wagon.

Reality dictates, however, that much misconduct does not lend itself easily to natural or logical consequences.

What is crime-fitting discipline for disrespect? A written apology or essay? As we have seen, experts and teachers consider writing for punishment a graphic no-no. What about time-out? Possibly, but it isn't much related to disrespect. Neither is a loss of a privilege. Or early bedtime.

Sibling squabbling? Mutual apologies are a logical first step. What then? No contact allowed within spitting distance of each other for an hour, day, two years? This could just as easily be a reward as a punishment. What about writing fifteen good things about your brother? Once again, this is writing as discipline. Though it would seem that such punishment is quite related to the offense.

Many consequences are neither natural or logical, yet they still meet the purpose. They teach a lesson: *You will be held responsible for poor behavior.*

Most day-to-day discipline needn't be creative and crime-fitting. It has to be simple and enforceable. To repeat Discipline Law 101: The easier it is, the more likely we are to do it. The more likely we are to do it, the better it works. The better it works, the less we have to do it.

Thus resulting in fewer crimes to punish.

IDEA #36: AVOID A POWER STRUGGLE

I agree wholeheartedly. Don't battle with Harmony on her level. Don't nag, argue, or yell. Above all, *don't let her control the direction of the exchange.* More often than not, such child-guided exchanges escalate, getting longer and louder as they progress, or to use a more accurate word, regress.

What exactly is a power struggle? Most experts would see it as a protracted contest of wills, marked by agitation and opposition for child, parent, or both. In this sense, "avoid a power struggle" is smart. It is a baseline for calmer, more resolute discipline. Power struggles undercut a parent's authority, rapidly chasing calmness and resolve from the scene.

Ideally, parents would prefer to achieve cooperation by using reason or persuasion, without having to discipline or to force the issue. When children don't accept our reasoning, we are inclined to reason further, leading to a debate, leading to a clash. Why can't they be more agreeable, cooperative, flexible—in short, more grown-up? The question answers itself.

The more likely outcome of a power struggle is Bliss's pulling us down to her level rather than our pulling her up to ours. We resort to her methods—words and arguing—rather than to ours—discipline and consequences.

Because a power clash can be ugly and ultimately futile, parents struggle to avoid it. The way they avoid it determines whether this expert advice is worth taking or ignoring.

• • •

Suppose Victor can't get enough of his favorite computer game *Power Combat*. He badgers for more time, disputes your limits, and stretches every allowed session. There's more combat at home than on the screen.

The advice worth taking is to set your schedule, stick to it, and inform Victor that each nag or objection will shorten his allotted time by fifteen minutes. A power struggle can't erupt without two parties struggling. And you won't.

The advice worth ignoring involves yielding to Victor's demands. Parents have told me that professionals have told them to lower a contested standard, one the parents think perfectly reasonable, as it causes too much strife. They are to find common ground with Victor. This will, it is assumed, reduce the number and intensity of the battles. Put differently, negotiate for peace. Reassess parental judgment.

I have three responses to that.

One, if you believe your game-time limits are sensible, why adjust them just because Victor finds them disagreeable?

Two, even if you do adjust, how long will the new guidelines be acceptable to Victor? How soon before Victor decides your new time is not enough time?

Three, are you setting precedent for future negotiations, not all game-related?

It is one thing to seek a truce if you honestly believe it serves the best interests of all. It is another to seek it out of exhaustion or second-guessing. Such truces tend to be short-lived, lasting until the next power struggle begins.

Avoiding a power struggle is fairly simple. That doesn't mean it's easy. Listen to your child's side. End your listening when you judge best. State your decision. Back it with consequences if need be. Refuse to argue any further. The fuel for any struggle is shut off.

—————:::::: SECTION FIVE ::::::—————

Miscommunication

Library shelves are full of books about how best to communicate with children. If only the kids would read a book or two.

As a rule, they see less fault in how they talk and listen to us than how we talk and listen to them. That's understandable. Since we are the grown-ups and assumed to be more grown-up, the burden to connect falls on us.

Thus, we are open to better ways to do that, including turning for guidance to the professional communicators. Paying for guidance, however, doesn't guarantee all of that guidance is worth hearing.

IDEA #37: DON'T ASK QUESTIONS

Don't ask questions? Why not? Aren't questions basic to communication? Don't questions seek information? Don't they show interest? Pardon my asking.

Is this advice pulled from some obscure theory of communication embraced by only a handful of professionals? On the contrary, it can be found in a high-profile parenting course. Schools, churches, and organizations of all types have followed its tenets. From a section on communication dos and don'ts comes, "Don't ask questions."

Again, why not? Because questions can be a form of interrogation, the supposition being that questions ask: Where does blame lie? And when so confronted, kids reflexively shut down, lawyer up, or plead the Fifth. Effectively, communication ceases.

* * *

The admonition has roots in client-centered therapy. It's also called non-directive counseling. The therapist does not direct the therapy; the client does. The therapist acts as a sort of emotional sounding board. She seldom makes suggestions, offers solutions, or asks questions. Instead, she empathizes, restates, and reflects the client's feelings.

Client: My sister-in-law is always making comments about my discipline and my kids. It's not like hers are anything special.

Therapist: You're feeling put down by your sister-in-law's intrusive opinions about your parenting.

Client: To make it worse, my husband just sits there and says nothing. It's as though he's afraid of his sister.

Therapist: You sense that your husband doesn't understand why you're so frustrated, and you feel betrayed by his silence.

Clarify, rephrase, but don't question. For example, no "Does your sister-in-law make these kinds of remarks to other family members, or are you the only one?" or, "Have you made clear to your husband how strongly you feel about this?" The intent is to gently nudge the client to find her own answers. The therapist is a bystander in the search.

While it reached its peak a few decades ago, this therapy is still commonly practiced. Not surprisingly, its approach has filtered into popular how-to books.

Is parenting therapy? At times, it might seem so, as there are parallels—listening, understanding, and empathizing. It can be pretty expensive, too. A parent is far more actively involved, however, and must routinely gather information—the *who, what, when, where, why.* A parent seeks answers out of a need to know, desire to hear, stunned bewilderment, or mere curiosity.

As a therapist and parent, if I were to shun questions, progress would not only be slower, but less helpful. Questions help me to fill in blanks, understand intent, and seek options with clients and kids. Questions don't have to close communication. They can open it.

Have you ever met someone, talked a while, and come away with an immediate positive first impression? Why? Looking back, you realize that she spent most of the conversation asking about you. For each of your responses, she had more questions, not to be nosy, but to be truly interested. You mattered to her.

In moving a tight-lipped teen to talk about troubles (or about anything), questions can show a genuine concern. Dad wants to know not accuse, to understand not attack. Of course, when a youngster is facing discipline, the most skillful questions, persuasion, compliments, or bribes may only get slivers of an answer, if that. A standard youth defense: Don't admit to being anywhere in the galaxy at the time of the question-worthy conduct.

Of course, a question can accuse in phrasing or tone.

"So, did you actually think I wouldn't find out what you did?"

"Are you going to talk to me or not?"

"How dumb do you think I am?" (You don't want an answer to that one, do you?)

When asked without intent to corner, though, questions are a natural and benign tool of communication.

One question, while not in itself negative, is routinely futile. That question is *Why?* Ironically, it's a parent's lead question when flummoxed by a childish stunt. "Woodrow, why would you paint 'Woody loves Ivy' on our deck steps?" My gross estimate is that 84.2 percent of the time the answer to *Why?* is some variant of "I don't know." The other 15.8 percent, it's a blank gape, as if to say, "What steps? Who's Ivy?" Uncovering motives is not child's play, even for a therapist, even one who asks lots of questions.

A more rewarded query is, "What did you do?" Even if Woody remains stone silent, you can walk him over to the steps, and if necessary, hire a handwriting analyst. Follow with, "What do you think we ought to do about this?" Of course, Woody is thinking, "What do you mean *we*? You're not going to scrub the deck. You're not going to ground you." While your questions are good, still they don't guarantee good answers. At least, you're not using them to place blame. You don't have to. You already know where it lies.

Any more questions?

IDEA #38: DON'T PRAISE

Experts contradict one another. It is this professional confusion that stirs up so much parental confusion. Not only does "Don't praise" dispute other expert advice, it also challenges the everyday wisdom that says: *Raise a child with praise, not criticism.* Though some experts qualify this, too. Under "criticism," they include once-well-thought-of words like *no* and *don't.*

What exactly does "Don't praise" mean? Don't compliment? Don't congratulate? Don't award trophies? Supposedly these are acceptable, though trophies for winners is fast becoming a loser. Positive words are still laudable, but they need to be nuanced, lest a child misinterpret them to his personal detriment.

By praising Fulbright for his A's, the theory says, you could imply that his worth rises and falls with his report card. Should he slip to a few B's, would your grade for him likewise slip? If you tell Babe he's quite the baseball slugger, could he come to believe his place in your parenting lineup will slump if his batting average does? In essence, will a child hear praise to mean that he must be accomplished to win your approval? Will he conflate his abilities with his self?

To avoid unintentionally giving such a message, praise should focus on a child's choices and preferences. "Baseball is your favorite sport, isn't it, Babe?" or, "I see that school is a successful place for you, Fulbright." I suppose this would also mean no more saying, "You're a great kid!" How about, "You really seem to benefit from having me as a parent." Get the idea?

* * *

For maximum gain, the experts say, praise needs to be properly phrased. Otherwise, you could bring about the exact opposite of what you intended—not affirmation but insecurity.

Are you as intimidated by the new rules of communication as I am? I'm supposed to be a highly honed communicator, and I can't keep them all straight. Maybe I should use a teleprompter when talking to my kids.

No doubt, a parent's praise can take a tone of, "Your greatness makes me esteem you more," or, "As long as you're really good at the things I value, I will value you." This is not, however, what most parents are saying. They recognize that their child is a blend of strengths and weaknesses, as is everybody, themselves included. Their praise as well as gentle criticism are building blocks for a child's character.

Then, too, to keep self-esteem intact, parents may think they need to compliment a child's every move, from wearing matching socks to not burping too loud in church. Such overdone affirmation tends to over-inflate young egos. It is more likely to foster self-focus, not self-doubt.

A key is balance. You won't convince Ace your love is conditional by observing he is good at something. Maybe he really is; it's not parent bias. Neither must you meet a compliment quota of one per hour lest he drift into self-angst. Honest praise won't tell a child that he must constantly labor to achieve more and better to keep your admiration, particularly so if you remind him that his abilities are gifts from God, to be used with gratitude.

Some experts warn against using "moral negatives," like *bad* or *wrong*, as they can bruise a child's self-view. Others warn against praise positives, as they can bruise a child's self-view. What's a parent to do? How about a linguistic compromise? "Your behavior is unacceptable, but you really do seem to enjoy it."

On second thought, just praise as you wish, without overthinking. You'll be better understood.

IDEA #39: LET CHILDREN EXPRESS THEMSELVES

Yes, we want children to express themselves—thoughts, feelings, frustrations. Yes, we want them to know we're ready to listen, even to what we'd rather not hear. Yes, the more open they are, the better. No, they can't express themselves however they wish.

Adolescent boys are notorious for one-word answers and wordless grunts. A full sentence can be an explosion of self-revelation. The common charge against them is too little expression.

Adolescent girls, as a group, are more expressive, with dramatic flair from looks and tone punctuating their words. The common charge against them is too much expression. Their picture is often labeled "attitude."

Nobody would deny that open communication sustains good relationships. So what could be the problem with full and free expression? The answer lies not so much in the word *full*, but in the word *free*.

"Let children express themselves" often carries the unspoken addendum "no matter how it's done." The reasoning is that connecting with a child's innermost feelings is more important than putting any limits on the airing of those feelings. Let a youngster vent lest she feel her opinions and views don't matter. In short, any kind of expression is better than no expression.

• • •

In a nationwide study of strong families, parents drew a straight-line correlation between expression and respect. The more respectful the expression, the more of it will be acknowledged, however tough it is to do so. The style of expression softens or hardens its substance.

"Mom [Dad], I don't at all get why I can't have the freedom all my friends have. Their parents trust them. I think you just want to show me who's boss. My friends don't even think you love me. I never thought I'd look forward to the day I can leave here."

Rough stuff. If it's said calmly without rancor, though, few parents would shut it off. Most would try to dig to the bottom of it, assuming it hasn't been excavated twenty-seven times previously.

When pushed by emotion, expression can get real unpleasant. My most regrettable words have burst forth during a surge of frustration. When kids are frustrated by our discipline, they're not reluctant to let us know what they think. And what they think most likely isn't said diplomatically. It's expression all right, but it's nasty expression.

A popular television show features family life in all its exaggerated stresses and strains. The oldest son is irritable, openly disdainful of his parents' ways and short on tolerance. Mom and Dad absorb it all with an attitude of "we're just enduring until he grows up or moves out, whichever comes first." The message to parents: Accept expression, however ugly, because that's how kids are at that age.

Even if you allowed all-out airing, how long could you endure it? Few parents can absorb unrestrained expression and not eventually reciprocate with their own unrestrained expression, as do the parents in that sitcom. No matter how valiantly we might pursue patient listening, something within us bristles at being the target of unbridled words and feelings.

Teens are particularly quick to accuse parents of stifling them. "You don't listen to me" often can be translated, "You don't agree with me" or, "You didn't change your mind in my favor." To convince a child that you'll always listen, you'd better be willing to always agree. "Are you saying you'd like to go to the mall unsupervised with your friends? Of course, now I'm hearing you." "Let me see if I'm on your wavelength. You want to use the car to take five of your friends to the big-time wrestling matches three counties away? Well, sure. Never let it be said I'm not an open-minded father."

What's expression, and what's disrespect? Try an experiment. Suppose that your teen sprinkles her self-expression with rolled eyes and peevish sighs of "Yeah, right" and "Whatever." Can you suppose that? For one month, copy her style with your boss, best friend, or pastor. If they should say something you disagree with, merely respond with a "Yeah, right. Whatever."

At the end of the month ask, "Do you still like me?" Will you hear, "Well, I do appreciate your willingness to be so open with your feelings. I feel it adds authenticity to our relationship. All masks are gone."

Yeah, right.

Isn't venting feelings healthier than stuffing them? That's one theory that goes back to Freud, who called it catharsis. To be sure, pent-up, percolating agitation can be destructive to the mind and body. But is the reverse true? Does letting the agitation spill freely—in words or action—relieve it? A body of studies says no. For one, venting can become a habit, a habit that gains traction with every frustration. For another, while the venter might afterward feel some sense of relief, usually temporary, the ventee doesn't. He feels emotionally slammed. Harsh feelings must be harnessed by civility.

Freedom of expression is not an absolute right. It's conditional upon respect. It benefits a child's character far more to learn respect than to learn to give voice to every oral impulse. The best communicators let children express themselves, up to a point.

You could talk to your child like a counselor: "What I'm hearing you say is that I'm not hearing you." See, even when "you don't listen," you're actually listening therapeutically. Tricky stuff, this psychology.

IDEA #40: SET UP A WIN-WIN

Those who negotiate for a living—that would include parents—know to reach agreements in which the bargaining parties get some of what each wants. Not everything, but enough to be satisfied.

Professional negotiators are skilled at their craft. Still, they only have to forge deals between multibillion-dollar international corporations. They don't have to haggle with a thirteen-year-old who can't fathom why she can't yet have a boyfriend, or a sixteen-year-old who argues that the state says he's old enough to drive. (Unless they have a teenager at home. In which case, their professional life is child's play.)

Win-win does have an appealing, "let's all just cooperate" ring to it. It harmonizes with other trendy philosophies such as: "Win or lose, everybody gets a trophy," or, "We just play the game—we don't keep score," or "Everyone is special." (As one precocious cartoon child answered his mother, "If everybody's special, nobody's special.")

• • •

Child-rearing would unfold a whole lot more smoothly if everyone involved—big and little—could agree most of the time. And that could happen, if only kids saw parenting through a parent's eyes. Call me a Neanderthal because I think I've lived longer than my children. Can I assume that you too have lived longer than your children? Can I also assume that in most matters—technology excepted—you are smarter than they are? Then it follows that you are in a much better position to set up a win for them. Not that they always see it that way. In their eyes, your win is their loss.

Suppose your thirteen-year-old son, Sting, is pressuring you to let him attend a rock concert with his buddy Ringo. You're flat-out against it. He's too young; adult supervision is nil; the scene is way too crazy. Sting counters that by today's standards the concert is wholesome. The group, Kids in Charge, has only two felonies and a pending drug probe. What's more, Sting is unusually adamant in his begging and badgering.

Some experts (probably those without thirteen-year-olds) would counsel: Set up a win-win. Find an arrangement that satisfies both you and Sting. Otherwise, Sting could feel resentful that his appeals are being inflexibly squashed, without so much as a nod toward compromise. Perhaps he could call you from his cell phone on the hour. (Would you be able to hear him?) Perhaps he could send a picture of all the kids in suits and ties drinking chocolate milk. (Photoshopped?) Perhaps Ringo's dad will go along and sit a hundred yards away. (He's so much cooler than you.) If the concert is still a definite *no*, how about a substitute, say, a trip for Sting and Ringo to three movies, their choice? After all, he needs to feel some sense of victory.

Here's a recurrent scenario. Twelve-year-old Celina has been relentlessly calling for a cell phone since age ten. Actually, compared to her peers, she's been patient. Most of them started pushing at age seven or eight. You've made it clear: A want is not a need. You will reconsider closer to age sixteen. Your idea of a win-win, not hers.

Fast-forward two years. Celina is desperate. How can you be so hardhearted when she is now the only teen in the western hemisphere who is a technological hermit? Indeed, my rough estimate is that 92.267 percent of fourteen-year-olds have cell phones, 82.497 percent with full Internet access. For two years, you've been resolute. You weren't nagged into giving up your parenting judgment. But, as Celina regularly reminds you, she is a "good kid" (She's not on drugs!) and she gets good grades. What more does she have to do?

Maybe, you think, it's time for a win-win. Celina wanted a phone at age ten. You want it at age sixteen. Compromise: age fourteen. Finally she is happy—maybe the better word is *appeased*. And you are too, sort of.

Why the two-year compromise? Is it because you rationally reconsidered? Or is it because of other pressure—Celina's badgering, her peers' parents who have already yielded, argument fatigue, relatives' opinions, and Celina's building resentment? As one mother said, "If it were up to me, I wouldn't give one yet." I asked, "Who's it up to?"

All too often, win-win is code for parent concession. If you believe your decision is reasonable, moral, and age-appropriate, stand by it. Don't second-guess yourself because your child is unhappy and is wrangling for a "better" deal. Don't search for a social or moral alternative in the hope of reducing your child's displeasure with you. The most loving, reasonable parents face children who are regularly displeased with their decisions. That is not a reason to renegotiate. In the end, nobody wins.

When do matters lend themselves to win-wins? When no morals or character questions are involved, so it's simply a matter of preference. Six-year-old Dawn likes to sing herself to sleep. It's not your preference. You'd prefer that she be quiet—her singing is bad. Still she is in bed (your win), so she can sing (her win). Shut the bedroom door (everybody else wins).

Standford asks for a one-hour break after school before homework. That's not how you'd do it, but his grades are good, so OK.

Food, clothing, academics, media, friends, social networking—all more or less have a lot of parental flexibility and thus a lot of room to let a child "win," or at least get a sense he had a voice in the game's outcome.

Again, where your child's character and safety are concerned, you parent to win. It's not just being a little flexible when you lower the moral bar. You are God-ordained to be resolute in matters that affect your child's well-being.

Win, and the ultimate winner will be your child.

Idea #41: Give Choices

By this measure of parenting savvy, my father was decades ahead of his time. He regaled my childhood with choices.

"Help your mother wash the dishes, Raymond, or you'll do them all yourself."

"Keep your grades up if you want your license—your choice."

"Don't start your fake cry, Ray, or you'll have something real to cry about."

Dad's idea of choices wasn't exactly what today's experts have in mind. His choices were pretty simple: *Accept direction or accept discipline.* To the childhood me, neither alternative was preferred. Often it was a matter of choosing between two undesirables. In other words, Dad set the terms, I didn't.

Modern choice-giving revolves around asking Wynne how she would like to cooperate, a sort of "can't we just get along?" interaction.

Picture this scenario: Mom is shocked at her seven-year-old daughter's self-selection of school garb. It's wrong for the weather, and the color combinations are nearly as grotesque as her nine-year-old son's.

Rather than say, "You can't wear that"—way too autocratic—Mom might present a less grotesque option: Do you want to wear your feathered shorts with your sequined top instead?" Of course, Barbie could choose "C," none of the above, as she's personally invested in her first outfit. More choices then? "OK, which corduroy socks do you want?"

The aim is to construct, in business jargon, a win-win scenario. Barbie gets some say in the matter, and Mom gets some cooperation.

• • •

Two risks lurk in this scenario, however. One, Barbie may not like any of Mom's offerings, no matter how creative. And two, more bargaining almost always leads to more arguing.

Granted, a child's typical day does incorporate choices. Homework or dishes first? Brush teeth before or after putting on pajamas? Tattle on Ken now or later?

Giving choices can weaken authority, however, when the parent puts forth a reasonable request, the child disagrees, and the parent renegotiates.

Can you imagine an exchange like this one happening at your house?

"Mason, it's Grandma's birthday, and I'd like you to visit her with me."

Fifteen-year-old Mason builds a wall of silence.

To avoid a stalemate, Mom compromises, "What if you just called her? Maybe an e-mail or a text? Her phone gets text now. I think she'd be happy just to hear something from you."

Mom may have avoided a verbal battle, assuming Mason accepts plan B or C, but she abandoned plan A, the one best for forming character by honoring Grandma in person on her birthday.

Seven-year-old Mercedes is whining about having to share the car's back seat with her brother. Dad seeks accommodation, "OK, Mercedes, how about if either you or Avis sits up front?" An option, assuming Mom won't have to yield her passenger seat. But would it be better for Mercedes to learn to sit next to her brother without being disagreeable about it? How about, "Mercedes, please sit quietly near your brother, or when we get to Edsel's house, you will sit in the corner"? Still a choice, but not at the same level as, "Well, if you don't want to do that, would you be willing to do this?" Some choices just are much better than others for teaching.

My father's choice-giving is still the best approach: *Act well or accept the consequences.*

Idea #42: Respect the Right to Privacy

A mother told me she stumbled upon her teenage daughter's diary while cleaning her bedroom. Moved by curiosity coupled with maternal instinct, she began to read. Within a few pages, the emotional shock waves hit. In her daughter's own hand was clear evidence that she was engaging in some very questionable and risky behavior.

When confronted, her daughter showed no embarrassment or contrition. Instead, she roared into high dudgeon with accusations flying: "That's my private property. You have no right to snoop around in my room. I can't believe you did that. This is why I don't tell you anything!"

In a matter of seconds, Mom went from concerned parent to intruder. That shift was followed by self-doubt. *Maybe,* she thought, *I don't have a right to look where I wasn't invited. Maybe,* she thought, *I did pry. Maybe,* she thought, *I should show more trust.*

To begin with, Mom didn't deliberately root through her daughter's possessions, seeking incriminating self-testimony. She accidently came across the book. So the "prying" accusation is for the most part weak.

Daughter might argue that the prying began with the opening of the diary. This assumes that Mom had no right to know of her daughter's actions and whereabouts. Daughter would certainly like to think so, as would most teens, but the question is: Does a parent's right to monitor her child socially trump the child's so-called right to privacy?

• • •

Poor choices are inherent in being human, even in those who are most mature. When humans are only incompletely mature, as is the most mature child, the odds of heading down self-harmful paths rise dramatically. So God gave children gatekeepers—parents—who are wiser (usually) and who can steer them down good paths or close bad paths altogether. If those gatekeepers question themselves because of some trendy catchphrase like "right to privacy," who will protect the children? They are not capable of protecting themselves.

Understandably, children want an unconditional right to privacy. What better way to close a parent's watchful eyes? Liberty would then have great freedom to make whatever judgments, for good or ill, and to decide what to tell her parents when.

Is a parent permitted to be vigilant only up to a point? Only where the child, and some experts, decide is acceptable? Not in her room, on her computer or cell phone, or in her diary?

Another mother told me she chanced upon the journal of her thirteen-year-old daughter, Sarah. Again, while cleaning her room. (If kids de-trashed their rooms, we wouldn't have to be in there so often.) The journal didn't so much detail "what I did today" as it did lots of teen social and emotional "drama." Nothing too disturbing, more of a gripe session about how Sarah would change her world if she ran it. Mom and Dad talked with Sarah about the diary's content and, against her wishes, took it out of print.

Why? For one, Sarah was using it mostly to vent. *Venting emotions, contrary to popular misconception, doesn't ease them.* Through mental rehearsal, it tends to aggravate them. It can convince the venter that life is the way she sees it, even if in reality it's not. Writing down all of one's upsets doesn't generally help ease those upsets.

For another, without a wiser (read "adult") perspective guiding a youngster through her emotions and perceptions, who knows what form they'll take? All too often, the writing becomes a source for more troublesome thinking. I've yet to see any diary that had open lines for parental input. Sarah's didn't.

Did Sarah's parents need to respect her right to privacy along with her freedom of expression? Only if one assumes both are entitlements of childhood. If one considers them not automatic to age, but as prerogatives earned with maturity and trustworthiness, then Sarah's parents acted well within their parental rights.

All this is not to recommend that you stand ready to rush in with wire taps and search warrants, especially without any evidence of wrongdoing. On the other hand, most likely you have an overall sense of what your child is attracted to and capable of. Use your best judgment—sometimes it's a guess—for when and how to override any proclaimed right to privacy, or when to acknowledge it.

The "right to privacy" has an honorable sound to it. It seems so respectful of a child's social boundaries. Yet it is unarguably superseded by another right: the right to safety—moral and social. Well above any right to have secrets is the right to be protected from the results of those secrets. Both parent and child benefit when rights are in proper priority.

Idea #43: Don't Make Your Child Lie

What parent would deliberately make his child lie? Perhaps one lacking any moral compass. Or one who is emotionally disturbed. Good parents want honest children. So who is this advice aimed at?

Is it aimed at we who have dragged a juvenile accomplice into the web of our own falsehood?

"Answer the phone, Belle, and say that I'm not here."

"Tell your friend and her mom that we can't go Saturday because we already have plans." (Even though those plans are to sleep in, eat a long breakfast, and spend idle time on the computer.)

No, this advice is aimed at those of us who question a child about wrongdoing. As such, we are asking for a denial, assuming the truth would lead to punishment. Keep pressing for honesty, and we will only press the child deeper into deception. In essence, we become an accomplice.

• • •

So what's a parent to do? That depends on the circumstances. There are four possible scenarios.

One, you know the truth, and Truman admits to it. This is the best case. How do you know the truth? You saw what happened. You have enough evidence to make an undeniable case. Truman's younger sister showed you the video, along with signed affidavits from six of her friends.

"Tru, I know you snipped some of your sister's doll's hair. She showed me the strands left on the pillow. Do you have anything to say?"

You are not seeking a yes or no. You already know the answer. Some might argue that by merely asking this question, you open the door to denial. Since, however, you are stating the truth yourself, you are not asking for an admission. No deceit ensues.

Two, you know the truth, and he doesn't admit to it. He claims he didn't even know Barbie owns a doll. "Truman, I know what you did, so I'm only going to ask you once. If you tell me the truth, you owe your sister two dollars, and you'll write her a one-hundred-word apology. If you don't, it's four dollars, two-hundred-fifty words, and you'll do her chores for the week. Think carefully, because I'm going to accept whatever answer you give me."

Are you pushing Truman into a falsehood? How? You gave him two choices, you were clear about the consequences, and you made it to his clear advantage to choose truth. If he still denies, that is his decision. Further, you did not pressure. You asked only once.

Three, you don't know the truth, but Lila admits to it anyway. Where did you get such a child? Where did she get such a conscience? Instead of covering for you, she makes you answer your own phone and tell them yourself that you're not there. You couldn't make her lie if you tried.

Four, you don't know the truth, and Rob is not about to tell you. This is the most frustrating scenario. You don't know exactly what happened, and *this* child is not about to enlighten you. Mario says his favorite Matchbox dump truck went missing after he and Rob's last play date, but Rob insists he knows nothing about it and is even willing to take a lie detector test. Say the experts, if you haul out the bright lights and you and your spouse play good cop-bad cop digging for a confession, you'll only make Rob burrow deeper into his story, however fictional it is. In short, you'll make him lie.

What are your options? One, accept your ignorance, and lay the matter to rest unless more story surfaces. Sometimes parenting just takes place in the dark.

Two, seek further information to make an informed judgment. If you then conclude that Mario, not Rob, is more reliable, reapproach Rob.

"I can't know for sure what happened, but I know enough. So, if I'm wrong, I'm sorry, but I'm only going to ask you once…" Then give your consequences for truth or deceit, making those for deceit stiffer. Are you inducing Rob to lie? Only if he wants a heavier penalty for doing so. Again, you are making it in his best interests to be truthful.

Sometimes in desperation, parents will promise, "If you just tell me what you did, you won't be in trouble." That can prompt an admission, but even with a "get out of jail free" card, some kids still admit to nothing more than being somewhere on the continent at the time of the infraction. They can't take the chance you'll rethink your promise after you hear how badly they acted.

Such a promise also risks setting a precedent. If Freeman knows he could get a sweetheart deal by holding out long enough, he could pursue the same course in the future. Worked once…

• • •

Parenting has more in common with a civil court than a criminal court. We often have to act on a preponderance of the evidence. We don't have evidence beyond the shadow of a doubt.

Why can fabrication in the face of trouble be such a stubborn habit? One reason is the instinct for self-preservation. Your daughter Faith is appraising your volume, tone, and crossed eyes, and concludes that by acknowledging guilt, at the very least she will need a crack lawyer to be released from house arrest before her wedding rehearsal dinner. And her conscience is not mature enough to counter this instinct. That's why the one-question approach (used in the second scenario above) is relatively successful. It eliminates all doubt about what you'll do about an admission or a denial.

At play, too, is something called a "variable ratio reinforcement schedule." Stripped of its fancy language, it simply means "rewards at random." They are coming, but one can't know when or how often. The most potent reward schedule, it is how slot machines win players, thus explaining why some folks crank away until tendonitis sets in.

When denial escapes discipline, it is rewarded. It only needs to escape here and there to pay off like a slot machine, thus feeding the habit. Lying can be a stubbornly persistent piece of misbehavior, and to loosen its grip, a parent has to be more stubbornly persistent.

To summarize, when you confront a child, expecting the truth, you are neither coercing nor cornering him into a lie. You are giving him a choice. Whatever he chooses, one thing is certain: He alone chooses. To blame a parent for his dishonesty, however Oscar-award-winning his performance, is to misdirect responsibility. Parents provide the consequences. Kids pick.

Idea #44: Emphasize Quality

"Quality time" is a tempting justification. It asserts, "It doesn't matter so much the actual amount of time you spend with your child as long as it's good time." Make sure your face time with Tempus is as mutually satisfying as possible, and then you needn't be so concerned about its amount. It's the quality, not quantity, that counts.

No doubt, positive time is far better than negative time. If 61 percent of your minutes with Melody are spent in discord, you might be wise to temporarily cut back the togetherness. A little less off-key time may harmonize the relationship.

If, on the other hand, quality time is time spent enjoying each other's company, who would dispute that this is good? The more quality, the better. The rationalization lies in letting quality squeeze out quantity.

First, quality is a slippery concept. It isn't easy to plug into a timetable. And the older the child, the harder it is to get her to accommodate our schedule. Teens especially have so many options and so much mobility that their only open slot might be on Monday at 2:15 AM. Quantity time allows for a more open schedule.

Second, quality time all too often means entertainment time, as we plan some activity with Melody to share the experience. Quality, however, comes in many guises. In my study of strong families, a now-grown daughter remembered her time with her father. She didn't pinpoint particular activities or events. Rather, he was "always there." In the study, I referred to it as "passive presence."

One father recalled, "If the kids were playing in the family room, instead of reading my paper in the kitchen, I moved to the family room and read there." He didn't enter their activity; he didn't necessarily converse; he just quietly lingered close by. Some of the highest-profile parenting is born from what we don't say or do.

Our family had a tradition called cuddle time. The twelve of us would clump into the family room and watch a movie. Usually, one family member dozed off within ten minutes of the introductory credits. In my defense, I would last about four minutes longer than my wife. Once, I told my son Sammy, "Sorry I cut out on you guys so fast." He answered, "That's OK. You were still there with us." I doubled his allowance.

Third, quantity time leads to spontaneity. Unplanned quality—tackle football in the family room, sitting on mom and dad's bed to talk (watch out, this is a common bedtime stall tactic), a "Hey, Mom, can I ask you something?"—often needs quantity as its partner. One veteran mother observed, "It just seems to me that the quantity of time spent together increases the odds of those spontaneous quality times."

Another mother, looking back on many decades of family life, observed, "Parents and kids need more time to be bored together." What? Seeking quality in boredom? In a culture that is driven to move, act, amuse? I'm inclined to agree with this mother. Boredom slows the pace. It is a much-needed counterbalance to a society that seeks to fill every minute.

Common sense affirms that quantity time cements good relationships. So why has quality time gained such status? It's happened as a natural by-product of a culture on fast-forward. We don't have as much quantity for kids, so we turn to quality. Kids are flexible and resilient and in the shorter term will accept us skimping on them timewise. In the longer term, we can lose many somethings we can never get back. If our lives are overstuffed, there is much that can be rescheduled or eliminated that is far less valuable than our children.

Reality always has the last word. The reality is that time is absolutely indispensible to family life. It is the framework around which all other benefits are built. It takes time to discipline well. It takes time to catch a teen in the mood to talk—even to us, even if it's because we're the only ones around. It takes time to teach, pray, hug, apologize.

No matter how high it is, quality alone cannot form the bonds of a close relationship. That takes quantity.

Advice Not Worth Adopting

Adoption has raised its profile in the last few decades. Still, it is seen by many as making for an atypical family that is sometimes referred to as "special." Thus, navigating adoptive parenthood is also seen as needing special advice. However well-intentioned, the advisers—relatives, parents, professionals—offer ideas that may make adoptive parents needlessly tentative and nervous about their journey.

IDEA #45: DON'T ADOPT TO RESCUE

My wife, Randi, and I are sometimes asked, "Why did you adopt?" Simple answer: We wanted a family. Simpler answer: Randi told me to. Simplest answer: I needed more tax deductions.

The first answer is the actual one. It's also the answer of most adoptive parents. In a sense, we were the ones who wanted to be rescued—from childlessness.

. . .

The range of reasons to adopt is nearly as broad as the range of adoptive parents. Motives are mixed with anticipation, hope, speculation, anxiety, and reluctance. If rescue is somewhere in the mix, that's no surprise.

Nevertheless, assume that a main impulse to adopt is to rescue. The child needs a mom and dad, stability, security, affection, all the benefits of good family life. The parents-to-be have that to give. What could be wrong with making the connection?

Maybe the better qualifier is, "Don't adopt out of pity." If pity is the driving impulse, without a complementary prolonged perseverance come what may, then it would seem that the impulse could fade, as the demands of parenthood unfold month after month, year after year. When "rescue" is linked with pity, rescue will struggle to pass the test of time.

Some children do need to be rescued from their past and carried into a better present. What's more, it is those children with the worst history who most often need to be saved from their history. For a grown-up to recognize that and be moved by it is not some Don Quixote complex. To advise that an adoption should be rethought if it is colored by a saving mind-set is advice that itself needs to be rethought.

Many who adopt are moved by faith in God and a desire to live according to his principles, the primary principle of which is to care for the most dependent and vulnerable. Typically, that means children. Jesus says, "Whoever welcomes one such child in my name welcomes me" (Mark 9:37). Also, "Religion that is pure and undefiled before God, the Father, is this: to care for orphans and widows in their distress…" (James1:27). What better way to visit than to welcome someone into one's own home?

Is adoption that is inspired by one's deepest held convictions somehow less than psychologically healthy? Does it bespeak of some unmet, immature neediness in the adoptive parent? Will she be unable to maintain her emotional commitment once the initial "religious enthusiasm" recedes? Could it be that her desire to be a faithful parent also sustains her desire to be an exceptional one?

What really does it mean to rescue a child? The word would have to be defined in a narrow, almost self-serving way. Within a desire to open one's life to a child may also be a sense of saving mission.

If we call that a rescue, so be it.

Idea #46: Don't Adopt if It Changes the Family Birth Order

Birth order theory gets lots of press. Distilled to its basics, it says that children show identifiable characteristics because of their birth ranking in the family. The oldest tends to be more independent, achieving, and self-confident. The youngest, being "the baby," is slower to mature and reaps more attention. The middle child, without the freedoms afforded the oldest or the attention given the youngest, is the "lost" child. Hence the faux diagnosis "Middle Child Syndrome."

My own theory on birth order theory? It grew as families shrunk. Families now have fewer oldest and youngest children and more older and younger ones. (Remember your middle school grammar?) Not so many years ago, kids climbed up and down the family tree as another baby arrived or as the oldest left home. The birth order was altered by the natural coming and going of siblings. This alone would limit any effect of birth order.

• • •

Our first two children were Andrew and Hannah. Andrew was the older, Hannah the younger, or the "baby." Then came a new baby, Sarah, moving Hannah into the middle-child slot. Two years later we adopted Sam. Hannah then became upper middle, Sarah lower middle, and Sam the newest baby. Within a couple of years, Jonathan and Joanna, twins age four, arrived. Hannah now sat near the top of the age pyramid, Sarah (age three) dropped two notches, and Jon and Jo were upper and lower middle children. Sam continued as the youngest. Not for long, though, as we adopted four more children in the next few years.

With the exception of Andrew, who remained the oldest, these relocations resulted in different children being the baby, middle child, second youngest, oldest once removed, former middle, etc. Over time we had four different middle children, raising the question: How long does one have to be a middle child to contract Middle Child Syndrome? When Hannah was the younger of our two children, before Sarah arrived, did she suffer from latent Middle Child Syndrome?

When scrutinized by research, birth order theory is a squishy concept. It doesn't prove itself to exert much effect on kids. It's a popular idea, it seems to have intuitive appeal, but it doesn't hold up when critically examined.

Parents maintain they sometimes see birth order-related personalities in their own children. A more likely explanation is temperament. Children are who they are much by their inborn wiring, no matter their position in the family. For example, a middle child may show some impulsive, attention-seeking conduct—supposedly one characteristic of middle children. He probably would do so were he the oldest or youngest. It's who he is, independent of his birth order. A thought: Need a parent ever worry about Middle Child Syndrome if she has an even number of kids?

My wife and I did not adopt any child older than our oldest children, but not for fear of birth-order ill-effects. We were concerned about other effects. Older adopted children often have had poorly protected young lives, and as such are worldly, in a sad sense, for their age. We chose not to bring a child into our home who could introduce a history that would adversely affect our children, particularly the youngest.

Our twins, as said, were age four at adoption. At ages six and five, Andrew and Hannah weren't much swayed by the new "little kids" and their antics. Hannah viewed them as two more underlings to help Mom raise. Sam, age one, was pretty much oblivious, and years later, still is. Sarah, age three, was most affected. Jealousy and a few "you're going back" threats commenced. We addressed it a little at a time, and it corrected itself a little at a time.

If you are thinking about adoption, many considerations likely are present. One of those need not be shifting your birth order. Be assured, birth order has a negligible effect on sibling personalities. The more potent effect is not a child's age, but his previous circumstances. When pondering "what ifs," ponder the realities rather than the theoretical.

Idea #47: Don't Adopt if Your Other Children Are Against It

If you were hoping to get pregnant, would you first seek your child's permission? If you were contemplating a career change, would you ask her for a recommendation? How about moving to another home?

Changing the wall paint in the bathroom? Changing the TV channel? Changing lanes?

Admittedly, not all of these impact a child equally. (Changing channels might raise the most opposition, depending upon the program.) Still, the point is: Most big family decisions are primarily yours, your spouse's, or both. You are better able to weigh more of the relevant variables. You can better judge long-term outcomes. And you have a better eye for what color best matches the countertop.

• • •

A high-profile expert told a parent to quell her adoption inclinations because her daughter was opposed. She opined that the matter involved the whole family, and since the daughter's feelings were so strong, she should have a veto. She was ten years old—the girl, not the expert.

A child's opinions do count and are worthy of a hearing. Though this does raise the question: How many kids have to vote nay to defeat an adoption? Do all family members have equal say? If so, my wife and I would have risked being overruled after our first three children. They were little, though, and we were not above bribing them. Some M&M's, and like magic—unanimous consent for a new baby brother.

All right, our kids weren't that shallow. We had to offer a banana milkshake, too.

Most kids don't object strongly to a new adopted sibling. Some don't think a whole lot about it either way. Some are all excited about it. Some are nervous about reshaping the family, preferring the household the way it is. A minority are vociferously opposed.

Hear all opinions. Reassure, educate, persuade. If all else fails, try the jumbo banana milkshake with added syrup.

Studies reveal that humans—big and little—are not so good at predicting how they will react to circumstances that might arise. If an adult, with decades of getting to know himself, can miscalculate his future behavior, how much more so can a child? She simply has little grasp of how she will eventually relate to a new sibling.

As I've shared, our daughter Sarah, age three, had a bumpy adjustment to our twins' arrival. She started biting and acting up, and was unabashedly unfriendly toward them, Joanna especially. In adolescence, when Sarah was asked who was her best friend, without hesitation she replied, "Joanna." What a difference ten years can make.

What if a child resists the mere thought of an adopted brother or sister? What if she won't agree to, tolerate, or welcome a new sibling? What if she torments him, initially or longer? Her resistance to a "new" family may be understandable. Mistreatment of a new sibling is not. Stop her, with discipline if necessary. It is one thing to have inhospitable feelings. It is quite another to act on those feelings.

Suppose you do have to discipline your child for hostility toward her sibling, couldn't she just resent him more? After all, as she reckons it, his presence is the cause of her bad attitude. The short answer: No. Longer answer: If someone harasses another for any reason, does this help or harm the relationship? Not only will the first child recharge her opposition, but the new adoptee may start to retaliate, resulting in dueling ugliness. That will definitely slow any transition.

Routine, ongoing sibling contact in itself can soften hard edges. When siblings aren't allowed to clash, they have two basic options: (1) figure out how to get along, (2) act as though the other doesn't exist. Most kids drift toward the former, as there is too much proximity to persevere in the latter.

Other ideas: (1) Emphasize your child's status as big brother or sister in a now bigger family; (2) Involve him or her in some caretaking or, when you judge safe, decision-making; (3) Set up shared privileges or activities; (4) Permit the veteran child to show the rookie who's been ruling this block for the past several years. Just joking.

If you believe your family will be a better place for everyone with another member, then act. Trust that your child(ren) will more than adapt; she will come to see with her eyes what she couldn't see with her head. Once Brother or Sister has been around for a while, she will appreciate that she wasn't given the power to overrule Mom and Dad. All without a milkshake.

IDEA #48: TALK REGULARLY TO YOUR CHILDREN ABOUT THEIR ADOPTION

This advice reflects our culture's heavy preoccupation with self-esteem. It says that to maximize his child's self-image, a parent must make sure to emphasize to a child how unique and special he is. And no amount of effort toward building the child's self-esteem is too much.

Yes, an adopted child is special to his parents. Yes, the adoption was hoped for, pursued, and cherished. Yes, the parents are immeasurably pleased to have their son or daughter. But how much adoption affirmation is necessary, or even beneficial? When does the well-said become the over-said? Why does a child need to be regularly reminded about his adoptive relationship? Isn't the plain old parent-child relationship the real foundation of everything?

Another rationale pushing ever-ready adoption talk is that a parent needs to be vigilant against a child's feeling that somehow she is a second-class person, a kind of adoptive Cinderella. Thus, reiterating how treasured she is (especially at her annual adoption-day galas), how special her adoption was, how much she was wanted, and so on should lessen any adoption angst, spoken or unspoken.

• • •

No doubt, sharing warm adoption thoughts is wise. Can too much sharing, however, lead to an unintended message? Could it prompt a child to think, "Who are you trying to convince, me or you?" She may wonder, "Why are you so caught up in all this?"

The adoption relationship isn't based in biology, certainly. For that matter, neither is the husband-wife relationship. Most everything else in the day-to-day loving and raising of an adoptive child is the same as raising a birth child. Too much "you're extra special because you're adopted" talk can convey to a child that he is more different than he really is. Rather than boosting his sense of being a natural part of the family, it might lead him to question it, particularly if there are biological siblings.

Almost all adoptees see their adoptive moms and dads as Mom and Dad, and they aren't preoccupied with how that came to be and presently is. The everyday stuff of kid-hood inhabits most of their thoughts. The level of adoption celebration some adults think fitting may be much higher than what most kids want, need, or are interested in.

Adoption overtalk is an example of the expert tendency to overanalyze. At least that's my expert analysis. Are we looking too hard for adoption issues? We may think they're there; the kids may not. Why would we need to regularly reassure a child if we didn't think he needed regular reassurance? What if a child is perfectly content with his identity in the family? Perhaps his most pressing, immediate questions are, "Can I have more cake? And can you fix the chain on my bike?"

Sometimes a simple answer more than satisfies. One of my sons, at age fourteen or so, gingerly asked, "Dad, would you love me more if, uh, well if I were, I mean..." So I helped him finish the sentence. "You mean if you were born to me and mom?" "Yeah, that's it." "Well, who do I love more than anyone in the world?" "Mom," he said. "Am I biologically related to mom?" A smile flickered, and he answered, "No, you're not." Apparently reassured, he said no more and went outside to throw a ball off the roof.

The question never came up again, and from all indications, it didn't need to. My son got the answer he wanted, just the amount of explanation he needed, no more and no less.

Don't mishear me. I'm not saying to downplay a child's adoption questions or concerns. Also, I'm not advocating a "once said, enough said" attitude. I am saying—for fear of overtalking—that too much adoption talk can be as unwise as too little.

Follow your child's lead. Much of the time he'll let you know if there's something on his mind. Allow my son Peter to illustrate. He and I would regularly meet my parents for breakfast. I don't recall what my mother said to get his five-year-old mind turning, but one day as we were driving away from the restaurant, Peter began.

"Dad, you were in Grandma's belly when you were a really little baby, weren't you?"

"Yes, Petey, I was."

"Was I in Mommy's belly?"

Oh boy, here we go. And I'm in the car without my wife. Well, I guess now's as good a time as any to talk.

"No, Petey, you weren't. You were in another mommy's belly."

Silence. He was processing. Maybe he would process long enough for me to get home and find Randi. No chance.

"How did I get in there?"

Great. I just dodged the adoption talk only to face the facts-of-life talk. When stymied, seek clarification.

"What do you mean, Pete?"

"You know, who put me in there?"

An accurate answer can always involve God, while ducking unwanted specifics.

"God put you in there."

"How did he do that?"

"What do you mean, Pete?" (I wholeheartedly advise the "What do you mean?" strategy for a range of parent-child discourses.)

"I mean, did he throw me down in there, or did he just lay me in there?"

I might make it home after all. Pete was just asking boy-type questions.

"Well, Pete, that's easy. He just laid you in there."

Dead silence. Discussion closed. Peter was satisfied—for one traffic light. Then came his grand finale: "Why didn't she keep me?"

I didn't have my cell phone to call Randi, so it looked as if I was on my own.

"Petey, she wanted you to have a mommy and a daddy, and she didn't have a daddy for you. So she looked for a mommy and a daddy. God knew you needed a daddy, and he also knew I needed a Petey, so he put us together.

Deafening silence, but this time a settled one. Then Pete noticed a big tractor-trailer hauling cows, and he started asking about the smell. By the time we reached home, I was feeling pretty full of myself. I'd handled the whole interchange without once saying, "I think you need to ask Mom that."

Pete had shown previous curiosity about his origins, but this was his most prolonged set of questions. I am white; Pete is black. While he didn't know much about the birds and the bees, he did know his colors. But until that day, he never pursued their implications.

Sometimes it's the sight of an expectant mother. Sometimes it's a black child walking with a white parent. Other times it's simply the sight of a baby. Almost anything can prompt a child's adoption questions. And from there, the kids will guide us into their thoughts.

Don't keep revisiting the adoption for fear you're missing something down deep. Contrary to what we experts might think, with kids often nothing is down deep except what's showing on top.

Want to make your child feel special—unquestionably so? Make sure he sees and hears regularly how much he is loved and valued. Because he is your son, not because he's your adopted son.

Idea #49: Realize the Need to Find Birth Parents

Based solely upon media reports and made-for-TV movies, what percentage of adoptive children would you say seek out birth parents as young adults? When I ask this question at most public events, the answers range anywhere from 50 to 90-plus percent, with most toward the upper end. The image has become reality in the public's mind.

Adoption specialists intone about the "unfinished business" and "need for closure" that chase a child into his adoptive world. Hidden within the child is a sense of abandonment, a lack of wholeness, or a need to know. The struggles percolate and progress. Once independent and able, the adoptive child will seek. The discord demands it.

• • •

So says the theory. What say the facts? The percentage of grown children who actually seek birth parents is under 10 percent. Less than one in ten pursues the supposed universal need to know. Of those who connect with a birth parent, the connection runs the continuum from short-term curiosity to ongoing relationship.

Perhaps more have the desire but don't act—for fear of hurting adoptive parents or because they're apathetic, unsure of what they might encounter, or concerned about legal hurdles. Any of these and more could inhibit searching. But for how many? Twenty percent? Fifty? There are no hard numbers, so we are forced to guess.

My experience with adoption, both personal and professional, is that if it looks like little or no inner turmoil is there, little or nothing probably is. Most adoptees consider their adoptive parents their "real" parents. Furthermore, the warmer the adoptee's family, the more warmly she feels toward her birth parents, birth mom in particular, even if she lacks any urge to connect, emotionally or geographically. Most adoptees derive closure and security from a good family. They simply don't report the adoption issues some "experts" propose they have. And I'm inclined to believe the kids.

My own children are now spread between the ages of fifteen and twenty-seven, with eight past the age of majority. Have we had questions about biological beginnings? Yes, and for each child, we had more or less history to share. Have any of our young adults undertaken a search for their birth parents? No, even though Randi and I have made it clear that we would not be threatened by it and that we would help them however we could. Our oldest son once told us that it would be very hard for him to imagine having any other family. His world was our family, where he was content.

Suppose he weren't so content. Could that spur the desire to look elsewhere? This speaks to what I call the "better parent fantasy." Particularly during edgy adolescence, a teen might vent his wish for different parents, or his wish that his parents would be different. For the biological child, this is fantasy. He's stuck with these Neanderthals. For the adoptive child, that "better parent" may be out there somewhere. And life sure would be better with him or her. It couldn't be worse, especially when compared to these "plan Bs" he's stuck with.

Our own child who has shown the most interest in his genetic roots also is the one who was most dissatisfied with our parenting. Interestingly enough, his interest in those roots abated when he became independent, living on his own without our rules.

The better parent fantasy can mislead a parent into thinking her child has adoption angst when he does not. "I'm going to find my real mom" doesn't always follow from unfinished psychological business. Rather it could come from a sentiment of "I wish I had an alternative to you, and I might, you know."

To summarize, nearly all adopted children view their adoptive parents as Mom and Dad and not as substitutes or childhood stand-ins. They may love and be grateful to the biological parents they don't know, but the relationship with the committed parents they do know gives them the sense of who they are. They feel little drive to seek, find closure, or satisfy curiosity. They know how much they are loved in the here and now, and for them, that is more than enough.

—:::::: CONCLUSION ::::::—

Idea #50: Don't Try to Be Your Child's Best Friend

I'd like to close with what may be one of the most prevalent bits of "expert advice": *Don't try to be your child's best friend.*

This doesn't sound like advice worth ignoring. It sounds more like time-tested wisdom. Most parents agree with it. It is founded upon the reality that parents and children are not equals—in authority, experience, judgment, foresight, maturity (one hopes.) Therefore, trying too hard to be your child's best friend can be the very thing that spoils any friendship, while at the same time undercutting your child-rearing.

Every parent knows parents who are consumed with being accepted, understood, and liked by their child. In short, they want first and foremost to be their child's friend. And the outcome is not pretty.

So how is "Don't try to be your child's best friend" questionable advice, ignorable even? That depends upon which relationship is paramount. If you strive to be friend first and parent second, likely both relationships will be rocky. If you aim to be parent first, friend second, likely both will thrive.

I can make a safe assumption about you. You are a loving mother or father whose strongest desire is to raise a moral, well-adjusted child. Uninvolved parents don't generally pick up a parenting book. Unless this is a gift from your mother. Which begs the question: What is she saying?

This whole book has been about helping you to be your child's best friend. By recognizing and countering dubious or bad advice, you will act with more self-confidence and authority. It's a straightforward relationship: A better parent is a better friend. And the best parents make the best friends.

Do try to be your child's best friend. Strive first to be his parent. Good friendship will naturally follow.

Anyway, that's my advice.